Growth Driven Testing

Moolya way of test and culture that has helped startups and enterprises grow

Pradeep Soundararajan

Dhanasekar Subramaniam

Foreword By Parthasarathy NS

notionpress.com

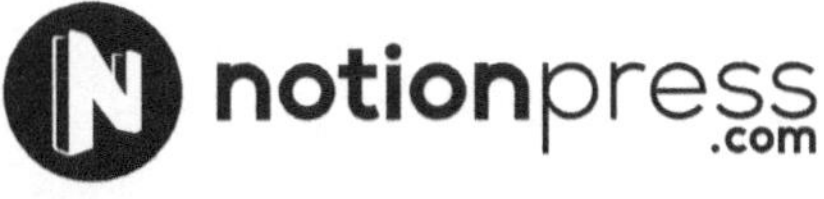

INDIA • SINGAPORE • MALAYSIA

ISBN
Hardcase: 979-8-89133-802-9
Paperback: 979-8-89026-974-4

Dedicated to those who build themselves by
building others.

We stand on the shoulders of people who have dedicated themselves to bettering the craft of testing, quality, culture and growth.

Contents

Foreword

Donald Knuth, the Turing award winner is well known to most computer scientists for his seminal monograph, interestingly titled "The Art of Computer Programming". This five-volume work is still considered within the computer science community as the first, best and most comprehensive treatment of the subject. The voluminous series was called "the profession's defining treatise" by The New York Times. While all this is known to most people in the computer science field, very few would know the controversy that it created in the usage of the word "art", when referring to computer programming. The Editorial Board of the Association of Computing Machinery (ACM) which is the world's largest educational and scientific computing society, described one of the purposes of ACM's periodicals as: "If computer programming is to become an important part of computer research and development, a transition of programming from an **art** to a **disciplined science** must be effected."

What is unsaid in the statement is the notion that there is something undesirable about using the word "art" when referring to programming and for it to make a larger impact, it must be science.

A similar description has been made for Software Testing – and various experts have written about the "art and science of software testing". Software testing since its formal inception in the 1980s has evolved. In the beginning, Testing only focused on ensuring that the software works as per the specified requirements. Later the focus increased to cover different usage scenarios and to find defects under these conditions. Over time, Software Testing then became a measurement of the quality of the development and slowly became fully integrated into the software development lifecycle. From being a manual and human resources-intensive process, it has moved towards automation. And more importantly, has become an integral part of the various software development methodologies and evolved along with it. With the growing complexity of software programs, testing has become a specialized field and much has been written about it.

This debate between art and science is a classic case of left and right brain conflict. According to experts, the left side of the brain is adept at tasks that are considered logical, rational, and calculating. By contrast, the right side of the brain is best at artistic, creative, and spontaneous. Without getting into a philosophical debate on this, it is logical to assume that we get the best results when we use the combined power of the left and right brains – and this is true for testing as well.

Historically, Testing skills and roles have got the raw end of the stick in the perception ladder of what is good work, in the minds of IT professionals. While this has significantly changed over the last decade or so, it is still a lingering thought in some, that Testing skills are inferior to that of developers. There are wonderful role models of Testing Professionals who have built successful careers and been the torchbearers of the Testing Industry – and the authors of this book fall into this category.

The authors give a new and refreshing perspective on Testing – instead of looking at testing as insurance against defects/bugs, they make a compelling argument of looking at Testing as a growth engine. Finding defects and ensuring that the software works in all scenarios is important – but this is just a necessary condition and not a sufficient condition for Testing teams to provide enduring value to customers.

Looking at Testing as a growth engine sounds good, but it is easier said than done. The authors share an experienced-based approach towards building this mindset in everyone involved in Testing.

Along with the art and science involved in Testing, the authors have given interesting examples around culture and leadership. Building a culture that is in tune with the business strategy is very hard – and it is harder to nurture the culture, and more so in times of high growth. Of late more articles have been written about culture than on strategy. Culture is difficult to articulate – and hence it is said that culture is how people behave when no one is noticing. It is like the fragrance that remains in the room, even after the person has left the room. There is a fine line between culture and cult. A toxic culture drives people and customers away very quickly. A good supportive culture is preserved and nurtured only when everyone takes ownership of this – not just a few leaders. The authors have the humility to share some of their own mistakes in building a good culture.

A supportive leadership team, who lead from the front differentiates the best organizations from the rest. A leader's job is not just to lead the organization, but also to build the next generation of leaders. And this takes time, energy, and effort. And there is no one-size-fit-all when it comes to grooming the next level of leaders.

Most destinations have different paths and different people choose different paths to reach them. This book articulates one path to build a mindset in people to look at Testing as a growth engine – irrespective of whether you are part of a large enterprise or an innovative startup. And this requires the art, science, culture, and leadership all aligned and pulling in the right direction. The authors have backed this with years of experiments and experience, thereby making this book a must-read.

Parthasarathy N.S.

Managing Partner, Mela Ventures

Co-founder & Ex-COO of MindTree

How to Read this Book?

Welcome to reading this book.

Why is there a section on how to read this book?

Putting a book out is relatively easier than putting a book out that people complete reading. Our focus is on value, in everything we do. Given that is the focus - we want to build help on helping you derive maximum value from reading this book.

It is an incredible joy for us that this book has finally found you. 9 months of journalism, collecting materials, assembling them, writing a high-level vision of the book, writing mock pieces, testing it out on some audience, gaining feedback from them and then building the vision for this book has gone into making this book happen. It was not easy to put together a decade's worth of work examples.

Post that it took 4 months of writing and rewriting many chapters to put it out to reviewers. Post that 1 month of editing and 1 month of publishing work has gone into putting this book in your hand. We have a reason to feel very satisfied that this book is finally in your hands.

Hard work doesn't necessarily mean value and quality. We recognize it. That is why we got this book reviewed by a diverse set of people ranging from those who are hands-on - those who are leading - those who are building - those who are visionaries - those who are experts - those who are coaching. Just to ensure your reading time is worthwhile.

This book is an experiential capture of how we built Moolya, its customers, its people, its culture and its leadership. This book also has details on how we approach testing and the value it has contributed to our customers. We have talked about our failures, how we recovered from them, how we course-corrected to make things happen and some part of the success.

Yet, this isn't a sales pitch of Moolya. This is an attempt towards a compelling vision pitch towards re-orienting testing, leadership, culture and people towards growth. The compelling part comes from writing this whole book based on the actual implementation of everything we speak about and the value and growth it has created for our customers. Equally, the compelling part comes from demonstrating that building growth doesn't always need to come at the cost of burning and stressing people out.

While there are certain Chapters dedicated to Testing - other chapters are dedicated to Leadership and Building Culture that are relevant to non-tech non-product role audiences.

This book is drafted in such a way that after the first chapter, anyone can pick up any chapter and start reading it. There may be some references from other chapters that they may miss but the miss is not going to cost the understanding of the chapter itself.

The heaviest chapter to read is the Chapter on Moolya Way of Testing for a good reason. People reading it may need to read a few pages - take a pause - think about it - get back to reading.

The Chapters on Leadership and Culture are going to be a lovely read for all entrepreneurs and leaders. The Chapters on Testing are written for both Tech Professionals and Product Owners. The Chapters on Fulfilment and Storytelling help Leaders, Recruiters and Marketers while still making it relevant for Test Professionals.

How many coffee, beer or tea sessions do you need to complete this book?

6! Some of you are going to disprove this number and we would love to know that.

Go ahead and enjoy reading this book. It is written in simple English. It has a readability score that suggests Grade 10 kids can read this too.

Purpose

In 1873, John Muir, an environmental philosopher, wrote to his sister a letter. One sentence from it became iconic, "The mountains are calling and I have to go." Similar to that, the vision of Moolya called Pradeep Soundararajan and Dhanasekar Subramaniam together.

Traditionally, Testing is seen as a Quality function in many organizations. This is evident in the titles given to people in Test roles. Even modern organizations that claim that Quality is everyone's responsibility have a dedicated Quality Assurance (QA) Team and titles in their organization. Shouldn't everyone in their organization be called a QA if Quality is everyone's responsibility? Ideally.

Hence, in practice, most organizations end up using Testing teams as 'Gatekeepers of Quality' or 'Hand Soldiers' to prevent some annoying bugs from leaking into production. Why would such bugs come in the first place? While there are many reasons for it, we have seen organizations suffer mostly from not having time (or the culture) to unit test, do deep code reviews or spend enough time reviewing their requirements and the impact it has on other assumptions made before. Most organizations don't need large QA teams but they do so, as a safety net. Safety against not having tighter process adherence and quality practices.

All this, according to us, leads to Testing being perceived as a low ROI activity or an indirect contributor to the growth of the company. We want to change that.

The vision of Moolya is to help customers get a greater Return on Investment from Testing by making Testing an engine that fuels growth directly – growth of customers, revenue and profitability.

To achieve the vision of Moolya is equal to scaling the heights of the Himalayas in 1873. Why 1873 and not 2023? Mountaineering has evolved significantly over the years. Today, there are sophisticated equipment to help people camp and keep themselves warm. There are helicopter services for rescue. Back in 1873, none of them existed. While John Muir did climb Yosemite, the world of testing and quality even in the advanced age of Chat GPT, is suffering the problems of 1873 and the mountain to climb is The Himalayas.

Equally, if Moolya wanted to do what the rest of the world did in the name of testing, it would be a walk in the park. Many companies have done it already. Setting up a testing service business is considered to be a low barrier to entry. Pradeep and Dhanasekar would have gotten dropped off on the top of the Himalayas on a helicopter. They shall see the peak. However, the joy in everyone's life is the journey and not necessarily the destination.

The journey to climb up to the vision of Moolya has been a major acid wash on their egos. Pradeep and Dhanasekar around 2010-2014 were super critical about things and hence, among the toughest people to work with despite a great vision and slightly above-average testing skills.

The mountain kept calling them and they had to lose their weight, literally and figuratively, to make the climb easier. Today, Pradeep and Dhanasekar are 2 of the most loved people within Moolya for their servant leadership to help people grow holistically and make unconventional decisions to bring value to customers.

What is so difficult about achieving the vision of Moolya to put Testing as a Growth Engine?

Changing an industry sentiment of something with a product is very different from changing it with a service. Moolya should have taken a product approach but it took the service route to begin with. Each route has its pros and cons. The massive pro of the service route is to work deeply and closely with visionary people at the CXO and VP levels. This has provided an insight into what it really takes to translate their vision to reality with Director and Manager level people who face ground reality challenges.

This led the leadership team at Moolya to understand why Testing is that indirect growth function and not direct to CXOs. This equally challenged Moolya to keep refining approaches to testing to make it into a growth engine for its customers.

How far have they scaled?

The good thing is if it was just Pradeep and Dhanasekar, they would have felt fatigued a long time ago. Today, there are several hundreds of Moolyans who are climbing this mountain, led by fantastic leadership and growth teams coupled with a phenomenal number of testers who think, test and automate. This has put Moolya as a credible story that is no longer a hypothesis.

90% of our business growth even today, after 12 years of climbing this mountain, is from existing customer referrals. Once people see the value, they want it throughout their journey of life. We are still walking. We have made walking at -30 degree Celsius, our comfort zone.

The real expert mountain climbers are the people who inspired us and the hundreds of Moolyans who implement the vision of Moolya, who are the sherpas supporting other climbers.

While it is tough, the sherpas have made it easy for the next generation of Moolyans to climb at certain places by putting in a hinge, and a hook, leaving a rope, and giving them snow boots. The sherpas also coach those who want to climb this mountain.

In the last few years, Moolya has seen rapid growth and we realized that to scale further, we needed to build a guide to scale the mountain and for our customers who want to understand how we do the mountain climbing. We needed to leave some practices people can do to make the climbing an enjoyable experience.

This book shall be a guide to help the next generation of Moolyans and Servant Leaders from Moolya to scale new heights. This book is a great discovery of how Moolya delivers value to its customers. This is a great book for customers to know the backend of the value they have been loving. This is a great book to know the failures and solutions to it on the path of seeing the success Moolya has seen.

If you are a non-Moolyan reading this, we welcome you to read about the journey. We either hope you would be inspired to climb this mountain at your own organization or avoid the failures we have encountered so that you *sherpass* us.

The mountains are calling you. Silence all notifications to listen to them.

CHAPTER 1

Pain & Painkiller

Pain

Any organization that exists today has come into existence to solve specific customer pain points. Without pain, to the customer, there is no service provider or product. Different customers have different pain points, and pain points vary at different stages of their growth too. Every customer grades their pain point for different levels of pain. The growth function is the hardest and most important function of any organization because it directly focuses on customers. Any function that is directly linked to customers and growth gets the maximum focus and budgets due to the complexity of solving the problem.

In that pain grade scale, many organizations hadn't put testing at a high pain and as a high complex problem to solve and had almost become a commodity. That changed with startups. To grow rapidly, they all started to realize that every function within their organization has to be contributing to growth.

The culture in which testing functioned across large enterprises had been slow, non-growth savvy, and the value was non-translatable to growth. The value at best of testing teams produced in enterprises was that of, "we have run through a hygiene checklist and things don't look that bad." Occasionally, when there were sparks of brilliance in Testers, they were moved to Business Analysts or Developers depending on their inclination of brilliance. Not many geniuses in testing were retained in testing to grow in testing.

21

To accelerate business growth, every function within an organization needs to contribute to speed and quality. Product and Tech teams needed to pull all their teams towards growth. Testing teams (that sometimes people keep referring to as QA and SDETs) needed to be reinvented.

Testing had to become growth savvy than checklist running machinery. Testers needed to prevent bugs instead of finding them. Automation had to become a service to Testers. 95% of the training material on Introduction to Testing we have come across on the internet introduces testing activity as a scripted approach, be it with a human approach or automation. This is also validated by the thousands of people we have interviewed and have gone through a training program from one of the many training organizations that claim to teach testing.

So, how can startups and fast-moving enterprises competing with startups translate test teams into growth-savvy teams?

Moolya – An Incidental Painkiller

The foundation of Moolya's approach towards testing is inspired by context-driven testing. Moolya's approach to testing is a derivative and a customized approach of Context Driven Testing.

Here is how Moolya looks at Context:

- Business context

- Customer context

- Product context

- Tech context

How could a tester have a background to credibly find business, product and tech context?

A few years before Moolya could happen, we were trained in Rapid Software Testing methodology by James Bach and Michael Bolton which focuses on a variety of skills to help a tester ask questions and communicate value. The founding team of Moolya practised the Context-Driven Testing approach and applied hands-on Rapid Software Testing across several freelance projects to gain some level of mastery, to begin with.

After founding Moolya in 2010, we were unsure of our service-market fit, up until 2012 when our pitch of context-driven testing started to click with many customers and we were too busy serving customers instead of recognizing what made customers click with our pitch.

We kept repeating our pitch and understood that the pain startups and fast-moving enterprises have suited our foundational thinking of testing. We intensified our focus towards this segment of customers. We became the painkiller for many startups. Once we delivered the painkiller value to our initial set of customers, many people in the startup ecosystem and a few enterprises started to spread the word about us and bring us a lot of referral customers.

It is our vision and approach to help our customers grow through testing that made Moolya a feasible startup.

Why are we incidental?

The customer didn't know to ask for context-driven testing as their need and we didn't know to articulate our testing thought process as growth-driven testing. Only in hindsight did we realize that we were aiding the customer's growth and that's why we were being retained and grown by them.

What value do organizations pay to a company like Moolya?

Customers pay to solve problems that enable them to grow faster. Period.

The leadership team in every organization is looking to grow their organization. On their path of growth are problems that slow them down and hence, they need to be solved. Ultimately, problems solved help an organization grow faster.

For a bigger problem to be solved, they need to be broken down into smaller problem statements and they need to be addressed by specific skilled people. A test automation problem is a sub problem to the main problem. It isn't the problem in itself. Also, the test of the worthiness of a solution is only realized when the customer feels good about it and appreciates it by either providing an increase in revenue, renewing a subscription or helping spread the word.

Hence, all of us are paid to help our customers succeed.

Our definition and understanding of "growth" is = Ability to add a lot of new customers + the ability to retain previously added customers + the ability to grow revenue (or a metric that matters such as active usage time) from previously added customers.

So, whatever we do in the name of testing or automation, if we are unable to tie back the value we provide to the growth of our customers and their customers, we are wasting time and have a risk of being delusional about our value. We may have a good pay and a nice title but that doesn't mean anything unless we truly understand the mapping to our team's contribution to our customers' success and hence, growth.

B2C Context

In B2C startups, customer onboarding is largely product experience-driven after marketing has done its job. The pain here is understanding the context of what blocks the user from going through an intended behaviour to convert them into paying customers. To excel with B2C startups, one must have an understanding of psychology, design, users, analytics, buying behaviours and patterns. No testing courses teach any of these subjects. Equally, most Testers want to learn tools because employers don't know to ask for growth-driven testing as a key value from testers. Everyone has got what they asked for. This is why 98% (I made that number up) of testers won't ever be good at enabling growth although they may be an expert at other things in testing.

The natural inclination for people in testing roles is to find bugs or automate tests. This is useful, but at times, not relevant and can defocus from what needs to be achieved. For instance, when Cred launched its app for the first time, many people loved and tweeted about the post-sign-up onboarding experience. Kudos to their product, design and engineering team who truly made it possible. Moolya was brought in as their first Testing team and we focused on what matters at that moment – experience blockers and not necessarily functional bugs. Finding bugs was incidental but not the goal we gave ourselves.

Similarly, Tapzo (acquired by Amazon), brought us in to understand the journey their users have to go through to book a cab through their app versus Ola and Uber. This wasn't a find bugs assignment – although we reported what came our way – but largely a mapping of user flows and asking stakeholders questions like, "What value is this step really adding to users?" We found something that wasn't a bug at all, was working well but was an inconvenience to the users and the kind enough team at Tapzo were willing to rework it out to make their users' life easy because it drives growth.

Even before Hotstar became a Moolya customer, during pre-Hotstar days, our testers went on BMTC buses via the most popular routes while streaming live sports over 3G internet to assess the performance of the app, the way the users really perceive it on the move. This report we produced got us a meeting with their Product Owners and Engineering Head at Star TV Office in Mumbai because their own internal test teams hadn't done that test. While they might have done other important things, building in complementary growth value is what we did.

B2B Context

In some B2B SaaS products, onboarding can be self-serve to some extent only. For instance, Bugasura.io is self-serve. Customers can sign up and start using the product without having to need any help in onboarding from our team. However, even in Bugasura.io moving them from signed-up customers to active usage to paying customers is a journey that is hard and involves some level of human involvement. This is where a lot of B2B startups need help to achieve the product market fit fast and then, scale fast. Testers need a deeper understanding of customers' business and their customers to be able to deliver growth value from testing.

Understanding a B2B customer is hard. Super hard. Why? Most testers can't relate. For instance, Hilti is a Power Tools company. Most of their products are bought by business owners who then give them to their staff who are involved in cutting, drilling and shaping in construction and other areas. Most testers have no clue about the customers and their persona.

Hilti from Malaysia brought us in to test an app through which their customers could claim a warranty, replacement or service. Our testers, hungry for context, went to a Hilti store in Bangalore and interviewed their actual customers, finding out why they were buying those products and what their needs were. The Hilti team from Malaysia were pleasantly surprised that we did that. Where else do we get the actual customer context? As a matter of fact, our testers found out why Hilti was such a loved product by the customers. Most of Hilti's customers used the word "reliability" or "durability." This was used by Moolyans as an oracle to report critical bugs and influence stakeholders to fix bugs that really matter to their users. Kind Product and Engineering teams at Hilti took our testers and their feedback seriously.

When the leadership team in Moolya built products and tried putting them out in the market, we learned half of what we thought was important wasn't important at all and the customers had different priorities than what we thought we knew. This led us to understand that Product Owners do have blind spots themselves and they commit to actively learning by talking to customers. That said, we also understood that testers who have no learning loop of customer feedback are less likely to be useful to Product Owners. So, how do we help them deliver this audacious goal to enable growth for our customers by enabling their customers?

Our customer onboarding SOP (Standard Operating Procedures) has a KYC (Know Your Customer) where our testers ask important questions to our customers like, "Why do your customers come to you? What do they pay for? What are their alternatives to you? What does your sales or marketing team sell them?" The answers to these questions contain powerful clues for our teams to know what is valuable and what problems we should prevent from happening and what problems are okay if they happen. We have to arm testers to understand business, product and technology to the extent they can be useful as growth agents.

The competition to Moolya's vision is not another testing company. The competition is what the majority is doing – not knowing how their work is enabling growth. We should never do that. As Moolya, we should always be focused on growth enablement for our customers by enabling their customers. That means we actively scout for problems that need to be solved.

CHAPTER 2

Moolya Way of Testing

Foundation

Moolya Way of Testing has a super framework and within that operates mini frameworks. It is for people to build within those frameworks. The super framework is:

- Questioning
- Visualizing
- Strategizing
- Performing
- Influencing

What is important to note is these are not steps or stages of our work. We need to question, visualize, strategize, perform and influence in every sprint, every new context, every release, every situation thrown at us. The super big mistake people have made in Moolya when we just give the framework (and not train them or build a tacit learning of the Moolya Way of Testing) is to think of these as a sequence of steps to execute. That produces the average value and not the Moolya value.

Questioning

Moolya value that we have been speaking about over a decade is no special from what we have seen test experts do. What do experts really do? They solve problems. How? Beginning with...

- Asking questions that matter
- Calling things out
- Getting answers
- Mitigating risks
- Preventing disasters
- Prioritizing
- Understanding opportunity costs

Questioning is the beginning point of all experts attempting to solve a problem. Questioning coupled with listening skills. Most consistent feedback about average testers we have heard throughout our experience translates back to a lack of questioning. Nothing else.

Let us explore what makes a human not ask questions.

- Lack of curiosity
- Lack of awareness
- Lack of understanding
- Lack of preparation
- Fear of being judged
- Lack of tacitness
- Lack of passion
- Inexperience
- Lack of energy
- Low self-confidence
- Insecurity
- Always wanting to look good
- Past trauma
- Imposter syndrome
- Previous employer bad experience

Humans are more complex than computers. It is extremely difficult to enable people to ask questions when their background has all kinds of baggage and karma attached to them. In Moolya, we want to enable plenty of testers to do expert-grade testing. So how do we do it in Moolya?

We have a framework for questioning and gathering context. It is the beginning point. People from different backgrounds, fears, insecurity, inexperience and lack of awareness have benefited from – no, not the framework – but by working with people who know how to implement the framework. Just the framework by itself is useless. We have seen it ourselves. Those people who had just handed out the framework and had no tacit learning from people who knew how to implement it had a shallow understanding of the context.

A framework enables people by putting them in a certain direction to prevent common pitfalls and short circuits to the progress they can make. Frameworks have been very popular in the automation world. Why? It is effective to give a start point, and have certain rules in place which by lessons learned are necessary, yet, offer a flexibility to think and script. The questioning framework that we built in Moolya has a similar thought process. We want to provide a direction and leave it to people's skills and curiosity to take over to see how deep they go to understand. Added on top of that is pairing them up with people who have been seasoned to ask those questions and also ask follow-up questions based on answers received.

Our framework enables people to ask questions and find answers about:

- Business

- Customers

- Product

- Tech

Actual Implementation

Here are some details on how this translates into an actual project. Cogknit has been our customer since 2012. The following questionnaire is how we began the engagement with them. Cogknit and its founding team loved how deep we went in understanding their context. They loved that we asked them important and fundamental questions. Presenting to you, our work from 2012 when Cogknit came to us around the first paid customer release of their then-flagship product, Nimit (now called iCog). Nimit is a personalized learning platform. Their initial target customers were universities but then, found success with large enterprise L&D teams.

excerpt begins

Pt	Questions	Anuroop	Asharaf	Ullas	Deepak
	Moolya	CEO / CPO	Advisor	COO	Sales Head
1	What are the objectives for this deployment?	Prove deployment worthiness of all major features so that it becomes replicable at 2nd and 3rd customer premises; garner great testimonial from 1st customer	End-user validation (on maturity and usage) of the E-learning solution in a realistic environment.	The product working seamlessly at the user end. Users are able to appreciate the features and its applicability. Realization of revenues from the customer	Provide an e-learning environment to the institution
2	What claims have you made to the customer?	N/A to me	NA	Following Deepak	Sold Nimit in its entirety without the ML component as of now

Pt	Questions	Anuroop	Asharaf	Ullas	Deepak
3	Who do you think is your customer?	Column F (Univ + college)	Educational/ Research Institutions	Extending 'customer' to 'consumer.' University staff, teachers, and students. The person paying may be the University but others are influencers.	Institution
4	Who are the stakeholders within your customer?	Column F	Heads of Departments and Faculty	Following Deepak	VC/Dean and faculty heads
5	Who decides the quality is good/bad?	Within Cogknit, me, Asharaf and Test/QA team	Agree to column C	Internal to Cogknit, it will be as Anu and Asharaf are suggesting. If it is at the customer level, I do not think that there is one person identified on the customer side. It will be a collective sentiment of the users.	User

Pt	Questions	Anuroop	Asharaf	Ullas	Deepak
6	What do you think is their idea of good/bad?	Designed intent and observed behaviour have to be consistent	First impression on the usefulness of the product decides Yes/No	Different stakeholders may have different perspectives here. University (VC/Dean) at a high level will wish that the whole product is seen as one that is utilitarian with less breakdown. Teachers and students will really want to extract value into their learning process. They do not have much support today and will appreciate anything that is much better than what they have. As I mentioned, features should be working seamlessly.	Click on any feature and it works in the first go
7	Who are the people involved and what are their backgrounds?	Whom are you referring to?	Seasoned academicians with PG/PhD background	CGQ	CGQ

Pt	Questions	Anuroop	Asharaf	Ullas	Deepak
8	What according to the customer is a "working solution?"	Concur with Deepak; As of today, I believe we have a 'jerky' working solution. It works ok, but doesn't look good	An E-Learning Content Discovery platform far better than Search-based tools would be acceptable	Following Deepak	They can use Nimit the way it has been explained to them by us
9	What is your idea of a "Wow" moment for a student using Nimit?	Rentable content + Rx Engine guiding him along a learning path	A guided, personalized learning content discovery experience combined with learner pace aware content delivery enabled through the RX engine	60 to 70% of their learning goes digital with the system providing help as and when they need it.	
10	What is your idea of a "Wow" moment at the college/ university?	Have to think about this	Opportunities discovery through Nimit usage data analysis		
11	Do you have a checklist for deployment?	Not yet - TBD	TBD	No	No
12	Do we have a logging system enabled to track usage patterns?	Yes	Yes	Yes, but to what depth and frequency is to be discussed	CGQ

Pt	Questions	Anuroop	Asharaf	Ullas	Deepak
13	Do we have a logging system for crash reports?	Don't think so - have to check with the Engineering team	Not yet from my understanding	I believe Anu and Asharaf here.	NA
14	Do we have benchmark/ threshold values you are monitoring?	What exactly are you referring to here?	It is a good idea	CGQ	NA
15	Has your dev team patched a problem in the production environment?	No	Don't think so	NA	NA
16	What is the peak load (users) you expect once you deploy?	Column F	Column F	You may want to go a little deeper here. 1000 concurrent users doing what?	1000 as of now
17	Is it entirely going to be Sanskrit content mixed with English?	Column F	Column F	Follow Deepak	Mixed
18	What is the background of real users? Have they used computers?	Column F	Yes	Follow Deepak	PG students/ Yes
19	Do you have a help file? FAQ? Support docs? How will users find answers to questions they have?	Column F	Column F, we need them	No	No

Pt	Questions	Anuroop	Asharaf	Ullas	Deepak
20	Do you plan for online support for users struggling to do something?	Column F	Column F	In the short term (till the completion of deployment), we can sustain with one or two associates there. In the long run, we are planning to have online support. Requirements should be high till the platform stabilizes and then come down over a period of time. This is my assessment of deployment for each University/ Institution	I am planning to deploy an MCA resource to help on the spot. He will be trained by us
21	How does a user provide feedback?	No channel in the system for this currently	Feedback on experience is captured in Nimit as user Likes/ Dislikes (micro level). Macro level feedback mechanism needs to be thought about	Feedback on the product? We will have to integrate that into the system if we are talking about product feedback.	Through the system as well as our person on the venue
22	What are things you as key stakeholders intend to do when your engineering team is doing the tech part?	Not clear what you mean	Academic content curation, mash-up content generation, and support Engineering team with new user data.	CGQ	CGQ

Pt	Questions	Anuroop	Asharaf	Ullas	Deepak
23	Have you identified the set of tests you/we need to run once a deployment has happened to determine if there is a red flag somewhere?	We need to catch red-flag items before we deploy	Agree to column C	No	NA
24	What problems of the users do you think Nimit solves and how do you plan to track if it really does that for them?	Raise the bar of education delivery; Impact measurement over a period of 6 months at deployed places. We have a set of guidelines and metrics for this — it is a discipline by itself	Agree to column C	This needs a f2f conversation, words may not exactly describe it for you.	Nimit will solve multiple problems. Difficult to answer here. We can talk this out.
25	How often do you plan to track it?		TBD	CGQ	
26	What are your criteria for success of this specific deployment?	Defined features working at satisfactory levels with no jarring UX/UI defects	End-user satisfaction	All features deployed to be working to the extent that the users continue to use them.	All features working once deployment is over

Pt	Questions	Anuroop	Asharaf	Ullas	Deepak
27	When would we get to know we are successful?	I am not clear on this in my own mind	A satisfied customer helping us to get a few more	I get a call for an extension of the product for next year	The user has to certify
28	What are things you are not sure Nimit can do right now (based on what you promised it would do)	The mashup is downright bad. The social layer and events/ opportunities are not up to the mark yet in providing user value	Agree to column C	Along with Anuroop's comments, I have not seen user-specific recommendations made yet. That is the biggest sale and I know that it is WIP.	Anuroop to answer this
29	What are the features you are confident work great in Nimit right now?	Consumption mode (search + consume)	Agree to column C	Follow Anuroop	Anuroop to answer this
30	What not working in Nimit once deployed is OK news for you? (I know Deepak will be annoyed with this question)	Am afraid that is not an option - we may have to buy time creatively but deliver everything in its entirety	None	I want to further annoy Deepak, but we may be able to live without MIDAS-based recommendations	
31	How good an idea is bringing in someone who knows Sanskrit to help us test search/ research features once we get Sanskrit data?	Column F	Column F	Follow Deepak	I am working on this. We will need an external resource

Pt	Questions	Anuroop	Asharaf	Ullas	Deepak
32	What do you expect to hear from the test team to gain confidence?	Critical UX bugs sorted out	Agree to column C	Thumbs Up!	No bugs and the system is good to go
33	How do you expect information presented to you to help you assess the product?	Have to think about this	TBD	CGQ - You mean the test report? It is going to be less a marketable report that we need and more a certification that the product will not come down. We can enhance the report to a marketing document going ahead	
34	Deepak: How do you plan to evaluate the product once you hear "looks OK" from us?				I will use it to feature myself followed by some hand-picked people who are not a part of this team
35	If any last-minute code push is to be done, what is the protocol? Who all should be involved in approving it?	CD pipe comes into play here; I expect to be doing at least 2 code pushes daily even after the deployment	Agree to Column C	Follow Anuroop	NA

Pt	Questions	Anuroop	Asharaf	Ullas	Deepak
36	What can teachers do now that they could not without Nimit? How do they know they can do it?	Mainly their source of knowledge is limited to their own self and text books they refer to; Nimit opens up a whole new paradigm for them	Context-aware, personalized, domain-focused E-content discovery	Knowledge discovery, creating their own content, bring in a totally new experience into their classes. Along with this, they can harness the social network to discuss best practices, less on plans, etc.	Skipping part one. I have proposed a faculty training program to the university
37	Do you really want people to take the Midas test?	Yes	Yes	Yes, but I am curious to know why you are posing this question	Yes
38	Do you plan to have a tutorial people must take before they get started with Nimit? Remember Windows XP tour?	We need to have a video tutorial – a guided tour like XP is a good idea	Good to have a video tutorial	Tutorial (help guide sorts), training program, etc. We will have to package it.	A training program will be helpful for all users and later on, all new users getting on the system will be trained by the person who will be on the job at the university
39	What are the most powerful features of Nimit according to you and how do you plan to help users get to do it and build a case around it?	Rent + Mashup/ UGC + Rx engine	Agree to Column C	We will probably document this and send it across. This question came as a repeat.	Rent/EnO

Pt	Questions	Anuroop	Asharaf	Ullas	Deepak
40	What do you plan to show to your potential customers based on your first deployment and usage experience?		The smiling face of a satisfied Nimit end-user	We will collect user testimonials and create a marketing piece around the first deployment	NIMIT

*_excerpt ends_*

With the above approach, you would have your own lessons learnt but here are ours:

Stakeholders:

- Had their own priorities and things they cared for

- Had a different understanding of value from testing

- Had their own success metrics to care for

- Had certain things they had not thought through

- Assumed the other stakeholder must know the answer to certain questions

- Were agreeing with each other sufficiently (there was harmony within the team)

- Were using this opportunity to ask some questions about each other

- Were brutally honest and hence, a great team to work with

- There's that typical early-stage nervousness from founders

Customer and Users:

- Deans sign the cheque

- Users were Deans, Teachers and Students

- Each of them with different expectations of the product

- Teachers could create content on their own

- Students want to see a significant jump in learning speeds and curves

- Deans want to live in pride for bringing a significant change

- Most of these users may not be tech-savvy

- Needed more intuitive experience on the front end

Product:

- There is a minimum viable product

- Stakeholders by themselves know areas that are not great

- There are specific solutions in the product that must be useful

- Metrics in place to measure usefulness

- Is missing help and tutorials

- Needs hand holding for deployment

- Scalability and reliability at scale is an unknown risk

Of course, we needed a meeting with the architect to pose deeper tech and testability questions following this. Overall, the context understanding we derived from this laid a foundation for helping Cogknit and its customers grow. It is a great testimony that Cogknit has grown over the years and Nimit (now called iCog) is a product used in very large corporations such as Infosys to enable personalized learning for their several tens of thousands of employees.

It is mandatory in Moolya to start on a project only after context understanding and running our questioning framework, irrespective of how many years of experience one has in testing or in Moolya itself.

Why mandatory?

Given the importance of passenger safety, commercial pilots, irrespective of their extensive flying hours, have to run a safety checklist before take-off. They have routines and inspections before and after take-off. They run a checklist every single time they fly. This is to make them conscious of what they already know and not let their internal biases, pressure or a situation they might be going through in their personal life over rule safety checks. No Captain and First Officer can say, "We have been doing this for 10+ years, so we don't need a checklist." They do it. They understand the sanctum of why it is being asked of them. Also, their training is such.

Our questioning framework isn't a scripted approach. It is a beginning point. Those who just use just the framework end up with shallow context understanding and those who take it deep, enjoy serving customers that they feel a high sense of accomplishment.

Training and *Tacitness* form a core part of enabling pilots to succeed in safety. Similarly, the framework of questioning while available to everyone in Moolya didn't make a difference to those who weren't trained on the purpose of why it came into existence and how to use it by people who practised on projects previously.

Questioning Framework

When we translate expert-grade testing to non-experts and wannabe experts, simplicity is the key to enabling them. In Moolya, we simplified our Questioning framework as we evolved over the years and arrived at Questioning:

- Product context

- User context

- Tech context

- Know Your Customer

To aid the simplicity of Implementation and consistency in delivery, we use Coda.io – a document management SaaS platform like Notion and define the framework there. So, for every new customer and project, the framework template gets replicated. This then becomes available for people to use as a beginning point. This has its own advantages and disadvantages. The biggest disadvantage is that people treat this as a flow rather than an iterative process. So, we might consider switching to a tool that makes it a lot more intuitive to be used as an iterative questioning framework than to use it one time and forget it.

Screenshot of coda implementation of Questioning Framework

> Moolya's way of Testing

> Onboarding

∨ Value Delivery

   ∨ Context Understanding

       Product context

       Tech Context

       User Context

   ∨ Know Your Client

       Marketing Goals

       Company

       Competitors

       Stakeholders

Product context

"I want to work with testers who see my product not as an application but as a product" – Anuroop Iyengar, CEO, Cogknit.

Not just Anuroop but many Product Owners and Founders we have interacted with have said something similar. So, what do they mean by that? What's the difference between testing an application and testing a product?

What's the difference between watching a movie in the theatre and on a TV?

What's the difference between a first-class and an economy class on the same flight?

The experience!

The product testing mindset is about caring for the environment (customer, user, their situation, their problem statement) and the solution (the app), trying to see if these two worlds unite into one through a seamless experience.

Moolya Way of Testing is to be able to gather the product context with this mindset and not just the app context. In our framework, we separated out the user context from the product context. That might be sending the wrong message to think of the product as an app but the training and tacitness of the Moolya Way of Testing has plugged the gap. The structure of separating product context and user context is to enable focus on questioning and finding answers to each of these streams. If one does great work on product context but misses the user context, they have not got the product context.

As an example, Zomentum is one of the best startups serving a niche segment of B2B customers. They service MSPs - Managed Service Providers. They partnered with Moolya early on and built a great culture that enables anyone who is an employee or a partner of Zomentum to deliver value.

Our team dedicated to Zomentum did a fab deep understanding of their product context. Remember, we talked about the environment around the product as the product itself?

Product Context Structure built by Zomentum Moolya Team: 2020

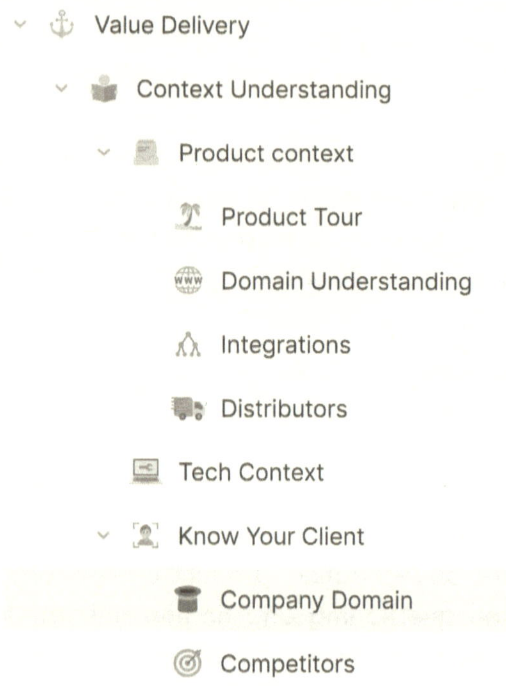

Here's an interesting example. Product Context gathering for Zomentum included the specific domain in which Zomentum operates (MSPs) and the integrations (because the people they integrate with also consume Zomentum's APIs and services) and Distributors who help spread the wings of Zomentum.

Why is this an interesting example?

That's because it was the curiosity, energy, commitment, ownership and passion that led this team to discover the information they did. The Moolya Way of Testing can take, at best, an incidental credit. Combined with the culture of Zomentum, this team enabled Zomentum's growth.

Another example

Previously, we mentioned that the Moolya Way of Testing and Context Understanding is not a one-time, linear flow process. Here is an example of an iterative learning and documentation of Product Context.

Unique Selling Proposition (USP) is what differentiates one product from another in the same category. Product Owners strive to achieve differentiation from the product they are building in customers' minds. Moolya Way of Testing incorporates fundamental questions about USP as a part of gathering Product Context.

One of the Testers who spent 5+ years in the Moolya Way of Testing working on a product we are unable to publicly mention discovered the Product Owner talking about a specific USP in a meeting that had not been captured previously and decided to document it and have it highlighted to other testers on the team. This enabled the team to focus on things that matter and move away from things that don't matter.

USP -> deep integration with our brand partners/sellers, as well as a one-of-a-kind seller site aimed at connecting stores to the platform. This will be a critical distinction in our ability to respond quickly and accurately to customer demands and preferences.

Iterative product context gathering: 2022

For instance, we have a Know Your Customer (KYC) as a step before our Testers begin a new project. This is a critically important step for our Testers to know about our customers and their customers. Those who are trained on asking Questions and those who do not perform are very different. We want to bring 2 examples to you. One from those who were not trained and were given the framework and others who were trained and then given the framework.

Here's people's work without training.

excerpt begins

Business

Types of Users:

- Employees of Enterprises - Customer-facing applications

- Enterprises and Corporates - HR Dashboards

*_excerpt ends_*

That's an exact copy-paste from a project. Now, at a high level, they are right. The users of that product were building for Employees of Enterprises. However, what is the real user context there?

Here is how people who are trained to some level on Moolya Way of Testing, mapped the types of users for a certain customer.

*_excerpt begins_*

Types of Users

1. Guest users

2. Logged in users

3. Users with a wallet balance

4. Users with vouchers

5. Supported mobile numbers and email to log in

    - International phone number

    - Valid email id

6. Inactive users

7. Fraud users

8. Targeting users by rules:

    - Individual User

    - Custom Rules

    - Segmentation by Profile

    - Default rule/Fall-through

*_excerpt ends_*

While the above is better than the previous, there's still plenty of user context missing. We will come to that later, but we certainly identified that training, passion and energy make a difference in what people do to understand the context. For instance, identifying fraud users as a type of user is an important point here to build tests that prevent these fraud users from gaining access to certain areas. The definition of fraud may not be people who hack but those who request for refund despite receiving a product or service.

Similarly, identifying an Inactive User as a type of user matters. When inactive users suddenly wake up and want to use the platform, their app on the front end has not been updated for a while. What should work for them and what should not? How should the product handle something that should not work for them and still get them back as an active user?

Such testers do great work on projects and ask questions that matter for growth. If the company is going through a user churn, reactivating passive users is a strategy to keep the growth going well. Testers who identify such a user category will ask questions and put tests that matter to build growth by enabling people to give users who are passive to become active users again.

What about testers enabling marketing ROI? Sounds too audacious?

Expecting people who never ran an ad campaign to ask critical questions to senior marketing folks isn't just ambitious but foolish. We agree. However, it is possible, with training and having a period of shadowing experts. This is how Moolya built its value at scale with the help of training and tacitness. People were trained by experts and they also observed how experts implemented it practically on certain projects.

When we did a UX study for Tapzo (acquired by Amazon), they were a few weeks before their first TVC. They weren't worried about downloads (because it would happen with the TVC) but something else. Ankur Singla, CEO, Tapzo said, "I want to learn how the First Time User Experiences (FTUE) my app and what can we do to prevent our users from uninstalling right after their FTUE."

The cost of marketing is super high but the cost of retention is much higher. All leaders in a product startup know the importance of FTUE. Cred focussed a lot on it. Something that blocks the FTUE is the most critical bug in Cred and other startups too.

How can young testers even know to test for FTUE?

By asking questions.

If we put humans in a game where soft fluffy balls are thrown at them – Green, Blue and Red in colour – and we ask them to catch only red, their mind fires up to spot red and be very attentive towards it. Irrespective of how young or old a tester is, knowing what to find when matters.

Context is like a monkey. It keeps moving, unpredictably.

Even in Moolya, the most common mistake people have made is to think of Context Understanding and Questioning Framework's use as a one-time activity. Everyone can start great but if they are not consciously observing context changes, they end up producing average value. We have constantly corrected this over the decade by reminders that context can change with many things changing.

What makes context change all the time?

From our experience of working with 200+ customers, we have all possible scenarios where context changes. We can classify them into macro context changes and micro context changes.

Macro context changes

1. Leadership change

   When a leader moves on and a new one replaces them, the context understanding should be reset. This has happened many times but here is a specific example from 2017. We worked with a customer that had 2 engineering leaders come and go within a span of 1 year. Each of them had a very different opinion on what kind of automation is valuable for the organization. This can happen due to a reorg too.

   While our one eye was always focused on what their customers could benefit from, we re-assessed the context with the new leader, checking on what their vision was. When a context reset happens, we are starting fresh. Only when we don't acknowledge it, do we end up being average. Our duty, also as risk advisors, was to caution them of the changes to time to value with change of approach. Thankfully, our scripts are still running (of course, we have continued to maintain them as needed) and they have been able to get a leader who knows that long-term is where the value is.

2. Funding

We work with a lot of startups. Every time a startup raises funding or fails to raise, it impacts the budget, speed and goals. When this event happens, our context understanding must be reset. Not completely. Here is a specific example again. In 2019, we onboarded a customer who had just raised their Series A. At that time, they had just hit the product market fit and were exploring the geographies that they should scale in.

The most obvious one was the US. However, between Series A and Series B, they found a better fitment with Asia Pacific and also found an investor for Series B who was more bullish on APAC than the US for the kind of product they had. Catering to customers in Japan is very different from catering to customers in the USA. The context switch isn't just for Sales and Marketing teams, it is for everyone in the org. Japanese people have a sense of quality that the world is inspired by their products. That said, every new Venture Capitalist coming on board can change the direction or speed of the company.

3. Pivots

Startups and even enterprises these days are constantly pivoting. It is a way of staying relevant and adapting. It is a way of finding a bigger Total Addressable Market or a deeper niche to focus on. During our decade-long experience of working with Cogknit, we have seen them go through at least 3 big pivots and 7 small pivots to reach a point where they have multi-million dollar revenue, orders and funding.

During these pivots, many MVPs were built. The context of testing MVP is different from testing a product that has achieved a Product-Market fit. If we apply one approach fits all, we would have slowed down the pivots for Cogknit and dented their chances to hit the orbit they needed to before their runway dries out.

4. Time

Time. Just that. Plenty of things change with time. If we do a blood test today and tomorrow, some of our parameters will vary. Change is constantly happening. However, for humans to recognize the change, it may take time. From our experience in Moolya, context is changing every month in an org. It becomes visible in some orgs over a quarter or two but it is happening every month. Those who catch the context change early deliver value; others are laggards.

5. Our customers' competitors

Around 2012, Moolya was the first to set up a test team at Flipkart Digital. Flipkart did not have a mobile app back then. They were launching their first app called Flyte. We were getting prepared to test and began gathering the context. There was a timeline communicated to us. We asked an important question as to why they picked that timeline. It was aggressive. "Can't we build better quality with a little bit more time?" Of course, Amazon was entering India just then. Flipkart had to get ahead, and hence, a competitor could seriously alter the landscape of timelines and goals.

Being change-savvy and not change-averse, we reworked the strategy continuously to achieve quality that was good enough for our first launch. Fkipkart's team was and is brilliant. We continued to work with them as well for over a decade. The team that worked with us on Flyte launch – while they went separate ways – carried us along. Why? They understood that our testing comes after understanding the context.

6. Technology updates and Regulation changes

Every time Apple releases a major new iPhone and OS package, many apps that were working seamlessly start crashing. This hasn't happened once but many times. This also hasn't happened just with the Apple ecosystem but with others such as Android and Samsung. While a crash is an obvious context change for people to respond to, there could be other implications too.

All governments can change regulations overnight. When the GST (Goods and Service Tax) rule was changed in India, many apps related to payment, fintech and e-commerce had to update their apps overnight. Similarly, with cards and banking, government regulations can change from time to time. The approach we take at Moolya is to first understand the change and then analyse the impact it has on product, tech and users. This puts us in a better spot to test.

7. Pandemic and global economy

   While pandemics happen once in 100 years, we have seen one in our lifetime. We have also seen 3 cycles of the global economy dip and recover. This has impacted our customers. Some sectors might be going through the impact in a bad way and others might be benefiting from it.

   When the pandemic hit, Moolya's e-commerce customers were gearing up for bigger demand and our travel sector customers were cutting costs. This resets the context. Going on with the same set of tests, approach to testing, plan and sense of quality may not even make sense.

   Some of our customers who anticipated growth in Tier2 cities only 3 years from now had it preponed during the pandemic because online shopping picked up in a big way. This put the emphasis on localisation.

Micro context changes

Macro are big things happening. Everyone can notice the context changes there but not everyone is good at analyzing the impact or course correction required. Experts we have worked with and seen in action are masters at picking up micro context shifts. It requires a level of consciousness to be able to spot these micro changes.

Why does it require consciousness?

A number of things are happening every moment in a project. Someone in a meeting is saying Yes to something and someone else is saying No to the same thing at the same time. This might look like just what happens in a meeting or a project but this Yes-No means something. When we don't pay attention to it, this creates a conflict in the understanding.

For example, when two stakeholders disagree and we walk away from the meeting without a conclusion from them because they are in a position of power, we are doing a disservice to a customer. A customer is at the forefront of the game. So, the Moolya way would be to seek clarity on the direction in such a context and advice if the direction isn't helpful to customers.

Similarly, micro changes to context can occur due to:

- Customer feedback

- An escalation

- A production bug

- A new use case being discovered by the customer

- Scope creep

- Last-minute feature request

- Team member leaving

- A new team member joining

- A Pull Request that shouldn't have been approved, approved

- A release postponed/preponed

- Some important things pushed to backlogs

- 100+ more

What matters here is to be able to recognize the micro context change and assess the impact it can have on the value we need to deliver to our customers. A micro context change can have a macro impact on the quality and value.

Visualizing

Sometimes, stakeholders don't know how to answer questions or they are overwhelmed with too many things. They need things simplified. This happens and it is normal. I personally go through this, and hence, can relate to them.

To make it easy, as Testers, we need to visualize our understanding through a mind map or find other ways to visualize and ask stakeholders a simple Yes/No question that is easy for them to answer. As an example, with Tapzo, we mapped the flows and arrived at 156 flows a user could take after download. It was mind-blowing.

I am going to make a claim and speculate something that may not be true. So, read the following with that awareness. In fast-moving startups like Tapzo, people would have lost track of the complexity they were building. Having 156 possible flows for FTUE is overwhelming.

Flow 1	Verify Number	Explore cab booking option	Location option is turned on	Auto Detect Pickup Location	Enter Drop location	Explore available Cab Providers	Tap on 'Settings' icon to select either OLA/UBER	Select Ola & Others	Select a cab from the list	One time connect to Ola	Register with OLA
Flow 2	Verify Number	Explore cab booking option	Location option is turned off	Request to turn on location Dialog Box	Enter pickup location	Enter drop location	Check available offers by tapping 'Coupons'	Copy Coupon code	Explore available Cab Providers	Tap on 'Settings' icon to select either OLA/UBER	Select Ola & Others
Flow 3	Verify Number	Home Page	Tap on UBER/OLA	Location option is turned on	Auto Detect Pickup Location	Enter Drop location	Explore available Cab Providers	Tap on 'Settings' icon to select either OLA/UBER	Select Uber & Others	Select a cab from the list	One time connect with Uber
Flow 4	Request to share profile information dialog	Explore cab booking option	Location option is turned on	Auto Detect Pickup Location	Enter Drop location	Explore available Cab Providers	Tap on 'Settings' icon to select either OLA/UBER	Select Uber & Others	Select a cab from the list	One time connect with Uber	Login to Uber account
Flow 5	Request to share profile information dialog	Explore cab booking option	Location option is turned on	Auto Detect Pickup Location	Enter Drop location	Explore available Cab Providers	Tap on 'Settings' icon to select either OLA/UBER	Select Uber & Others	Select a cab from the list	One time connect with Uber	Login to Uber account
Flow 6	Verify Number	Explore cab booking option	Location option is turned off	Request to turn on location Dialog Box	Enter pickup location	Enter drop location	Check available offers by tapping 'Coupons'	Copy Partner Coupon code	Explore available Cab Providers	Tap on 'Settings' icon to select either OLA/UBER	Select Ola & Others
Flow 7	Verify Number	Explore cab booking option	Location option is turned on	Auto Detect Pickup Location	Enter Drop location	Explore available Cab Providers	Check available offers by tapping 'Coupons'	Copy Coupon code	Tap on 'Settings' icon to select either OLA/UBER	Select Uber & Others	Select a cab from the list
Flow 8	Verify Number	Turn off Network Connection									
Flow 9	Verify Number	Explore cab booking option	Location option is turned ON	Request to turn on location Dialog Box	Enter pickup location	Enter drop location	Check available offers by tapping 'Coupons'	Copy Partner Coupon code	Explore available Cab Providers	Tap on 'Settings' icon to select either OLA/UBER	Select Ola & Others
Flow 10	Verify Number	Explore cab booking option	Location option is turned on	Auto Detect Pickup Location	Enter Drop location	Explore available Cab Providers	Tap on 'Settings' icon to select either OLA/UBER	Select Uber & Others	Select a cab from the list	One time connect with Uber	Login to Uber account

A snippet of cab booking flows mapped for Tapzo: 2017: Team Work

A critical thinking tester has to ask, "Why are we complicating it at this step?" and champion the cause to bring changes. Unless we mapped the flows, we ourselves didn't know that it would be overwhelming for the users. I love the people from Tapzo. When I personally looked at what they were doing, I thought the next step for them was to build their own phone. Amazon got lucky to get them onboard, but if that had not happened, they would have chased simplifying things for sure.

This isn't just the story of Tapzo. Moolya was testing the PayTM app even before PayTM became PayTM. The app was simple and had a limited set of flows for FTUE. Today, the app has everything. A user could do more than 150 things after installing the app. It has become cluttered to the extent that Founder CEO, Vijay Shekhar Sharma posted about how he is not liking the clutter of the app home page.

We use mind mapping quite a lot to bring visualization to product and tech people. This enables them to see what they are building and enables us to build some credibility and then ask questions to be taken seriously.

Bugasura.io app FTUE mind map

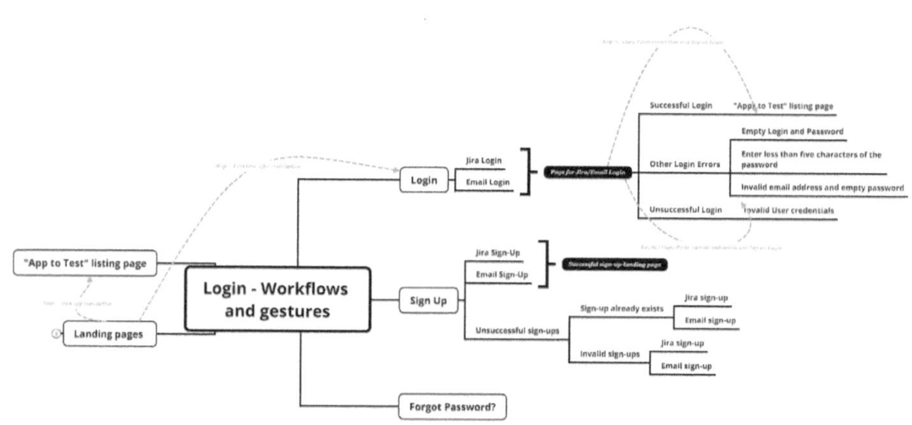

Mind Map of login workflows: Esha Medha: 2021

Bugasura.io is a modern-day bug tracker built for teams to move fast and close bugs. This is a product built by Moolya and is used by customers across the globe. When we were designing the flow for a Bug Reporter app on Android, Esha Medha, Solution Architect of Moolya, stepped in to help us out with this mind map that enables us to visualize and see if we are complicating or making our users' lives easy. Equally, this doubles up as a visual test document for testers on the Bugasura project.

After such a visualization, any Product Owner will trust the tester's test coverage to be holistic. With the attention span going down, a visual representation goes miles ahead of a full-text description. Decisionmakers crave for focus times amidst constantly being bombarded with meeting requests. Visualizing simplifies their life and makes them move with ease.

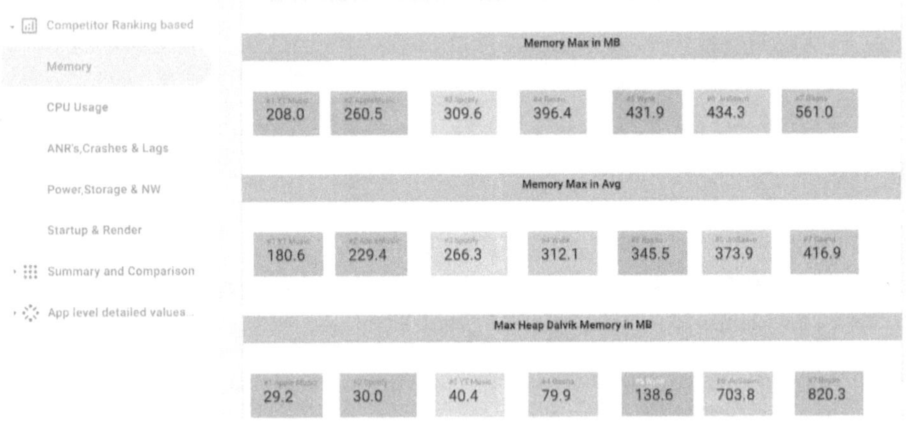

Competitor Analysis of Music Streaming Apps: 2022: Team work

A leading music streaming app company approached us to do performance benchmarking against their competitors and advise them on how to become the top-performing app in the category.

Our testers, of course, used performance testing and monitoring tools available in the market, but their context understanding was beautiful enough to enable them to think about what kind of reporting would help the decision-makers. They understood the audience for this is a mix of product and engineering teams. They visualized the metrics and set up a visual dashboard using Data Studio for product and engineering teams to collaborate and be on the same page.

In our journey, we have seen quality happen like magic when business, product and engineering teams work together as one. Given that we understand it, all our work is focused towards bringing them much closer to each other at every single opportunity.

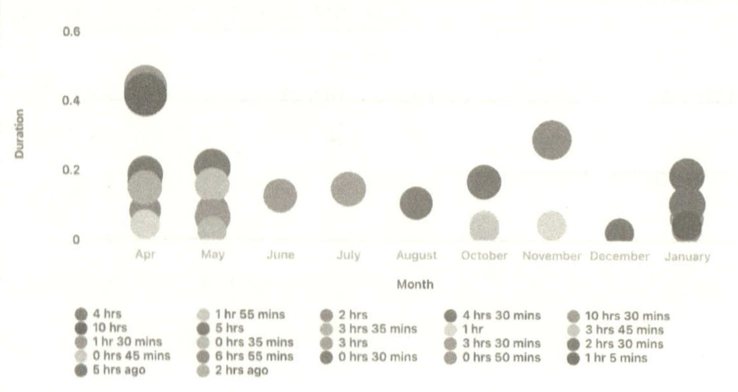

Enabling testers with the right test environment matters. Sometimes, no one wants to acknowledge the elephant in the room because it is in a dark place. Our testers put a visual and a spotlight on what's blocking them.

All engineers have to be problem solvers. Sitting duck on a problem by saying someone is not approving something isn't problem-solving. Putting this visualization is a highly influential approach to letting everyone acknowledge the problem and work towards resolving it.

In the Game of Testing Conference 2022, we asked this question to an audience of testers. "If a sales person is blocked in your company, is your company's progress blocked?" and their answer was "Yes." We followed it up with a question, "If a tester is blocked in your organization, is your company's progress blocked?" and their answer was "No." The answer should be Yes. We all know it. The reason why testers being blocked doesn't appear to block the progress of the company is because of three large reasons:

1. Testers' work is not mapped to growth.

2. Testers overcompensate to not become a blocker.

3. Testers live with the blocker until the org leader recognises it as a blocker.

Repeating this statement again. "Testers who can't influence are just filling timesheets" just to stress on the fact that hard work goes to waste if we don't influence people.

Overall Go NoGo						
	Functional	Page Load Time	Pixel Perfect UI	Measurability	Inter-operability	Security
Business Critical Path	Less than 50%	No Go	No Go	Go	Not Tested	Not Tested
Basic Flows	Less than 50%	Not applicable	Not applicable	Not applicable	Not Tested	Not Tested
Depth	Less than 50%	Not applicable	Not applicable	Not applicable	Not applicable	Not Tested
Corner cases	Less than 50%	Not applicable	Not applicable	Not applicable	Not applicable	Not Tested

Go No Go Dashboard built for a CEO & PO: Moolya Team Work: 2017

This project had a project management tool, a reporting dashboard, within it but it didn't provide a certain level of visibility to the CEO on are we good to go or not. So, we did a workshop with the CEO, CTO and PO on their criteria of Go/No Go and filtered it out to certain key tests whose results need to meet certain defined objective parameters.

As we ran those tests or those tests were run from a script, the results would start feed into the dashboard turning it automatically Go or No Go on the TV screen in front of the CEO cabin. Zero pressure on testers to give a sign-off or not.

Context is the central part of how we test in Moolya. So, the applicability of a certain criteria had to be visualized too based on the release objective or feature rollout. Visualization of context is as important as the visualization itself.

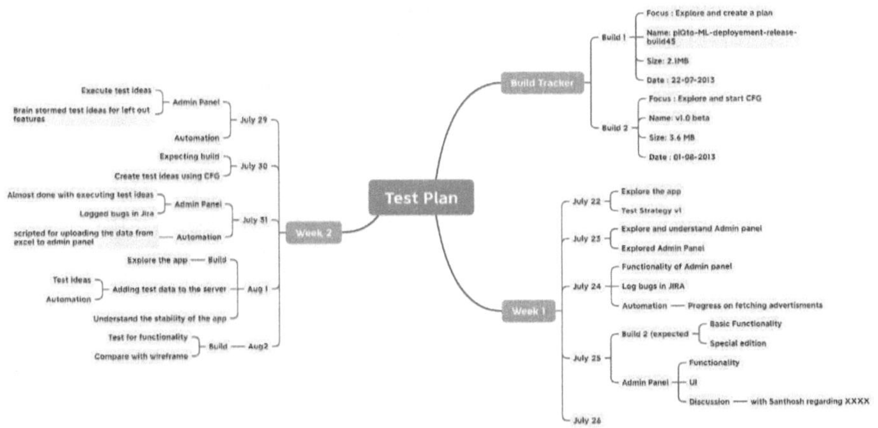

Test Plan built by a Lead Tester for self visibility: 2013

Building visibility to ourselves is an important and oblivious thought. Why should we build visibility for ourselves? We may know a few things about what we are doing today but we all need notes on how we have made progress and what we have not done to help plan our next day.

This practice has helped many testers in Moolya become conscious of themselves, their choices of test coverage and learning. Consciousness is the least spoken topic in IT. We strongly believe many experts who communicate everything required to be good in testing and boil it down to a "skill" are themselves oblivious to why they became an expert in the first place when everyone else had the access to the same skills they had to.

Building visibility to ourselves is the first step towards consciousness. It is like recording a video of ours. We become too conscious of ourselves. It challenges us with the perception of how we look and how we speak and our understanding of our body language. It is uncomfortable initially, but over a period of time, we build the comfort of knowing what we have done, how we have done and why we have done certain things in a certain way.

Strategizing

Strategy means plenty of things to plenty of people. Most often, a strategy document is drafted in a way that the audience finds it hard to comprehend what the strategy really is. This then forces a meeting where people who wrote the documentation have to explain what is in the document.

Making things simple is the way for anyone in this world to translate an understanding into reality. How do people make complex things simple?

Two things:

- Slow thinking

- Deep thinking

- Practicing simplicity

Deep thinking

Shallow thinking is easy. Why? Most people do it. For instance, benchmarking an application against competitors is a necessary step every product has to go through. Some products go through fierce competition. Benchmarking then becomes a frequent activity. How can testers really do this? Do they really understand business and competition?

Most testers don't.

Deep-thinking testers do.

Deep thinking requires time. Not to think but to prepare.

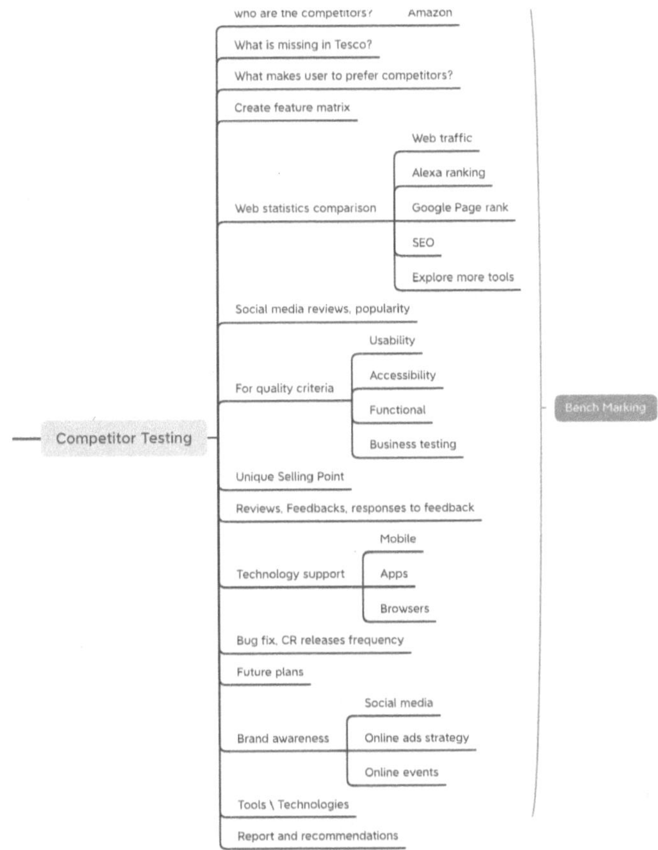

Capture of brainstorming between testers tasked to build competitor benchmarking for Tesco: 2012

In the above example that was WIP, this is the first version draft testers produced. The report that is unavailable to publish had an in-depth analysis and as a part of building this further, the testers collaborated with business, product and tech teams.

Product Coverage Outline (PCO)

The smartest of the testers not only want to provide early feedback but also want to get early feedback on their understanding and their coverage plan. This should not be mistaken for what most low-confidence people do. They think they need approval from stakeholders to do things they know they should be doing. Sometimes, stakeholders can provide feedback and other times, they may not be able to.

For instance, a Product Owner or a Business Analyst might be interested to know the plan for testing a specific story but may not always have the time to go through the details of the same. This is why Moolya focuses on mind maps that help the stakeholders have a quicker and easier way to digest what the understanding is and what will be done to achieve the desired result. Product Owners are keen to understand if the tester shall cover everything that the customer is going to touch.

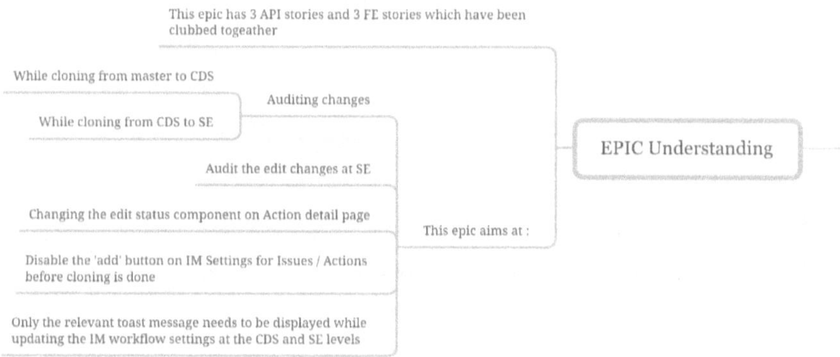

Epic understanding sample from a project: 2018

When POs and BAs gain confidence in their understanding, the credibility they associate with a tester reporting a certain bug is incredibly high. This is an important step in influencing stakeholders. Stakeholders are careful about whom they choose to be influenced by. Epic understanding is a small piece of the puzzle.

Product Coverage Outline (PCO) helps capture the strategy and answers questions stakeholders often have to understand what is being tested and gain confidence that important things that matter are being covered.

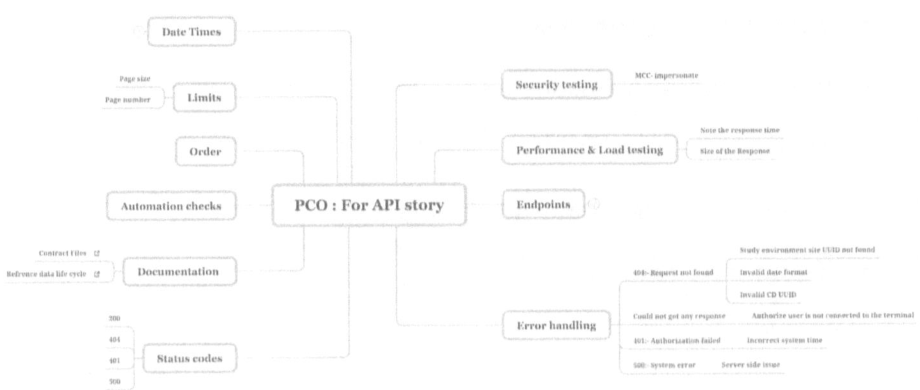

Product Coverage Outline for a story that involves API: 2017

The quantum of unmaintainable and incomprehensible documentation that happens in the world of testing is humungous. Mind Maps have always come in very handy for us to help build maintainable and comprehensible documentation. Equally, it makes stakeholders' jobs easy to read and provide feedback.

The mind maps are only useful if they are a derivative of a tester having asked questions, clarified assumptions and refined the thought process. Sometimes, this happens during grooming sessions from Product and Business Teams in partnership with the whole engineering team. Why do we mention this?

When people discover the format of a PCO mind map, their lazy brain can make them think — here is a template to fill. The template is only useful after an understanding has been arrived at. Understanding comes from drawing useful information from several stakeholders' minds and from partly available documentation that may include emails, slack, text and calls.

When we observe what testers mostly did to arrive at a PCO that builds credibility with stakeholders, we see a pattern.

They:

- Understand the context

- Simplify their understanding

- Build visibility to stakeholders with a simple presentation

- Share their understanding

- Receive feedback from stakeholders

- Incorporate feedback

- Provide visibility

- Proceed

Test Coverage

While the Product Coverage Outline largely focuses on Product and Customer Flows and enables Product Owners and Business Analysts to provide feedback, it doesn't extend to detailing to test coverage. It doesn't need to. Test Coverage is a translation of a Product Coverage Outline (PO Savvy) to Testing (Test Execution savvy) details.

Typically in large enterprises, test coverage is considered as test case coverage that has some mapping to requirements and they spend a lot of effort to build traceability between test cases and requirements. In startups, stakeholders don't have time to review test cases or test documentation.

Moolya's approach to test coverage is to be able to capture different types of coverage and models that help in achieving the goal.

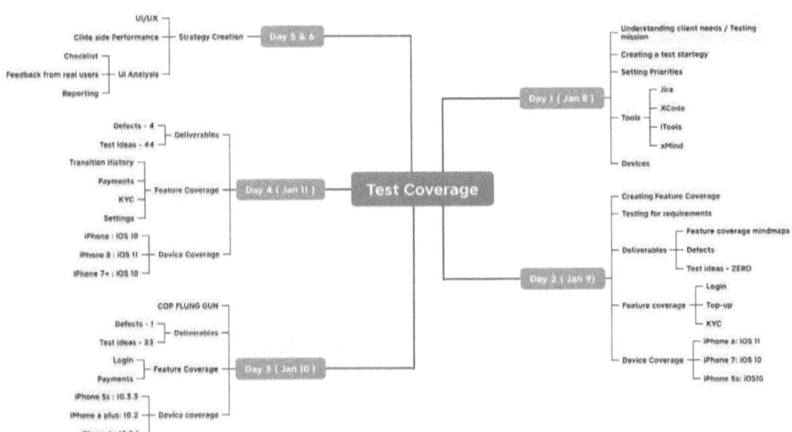

Test coverage report for a mobile application: 2014

Performing

When testers gather context and keep their focus on the value and growth of their customers while testing, they are performing. Otherwise, they are "executing" tests. Execution has two meanings. One, of course, is to carry on with a plan and the other is to kill. When people neither gather context nor focus on value to customers, they are executing (killing) tests.

There is joy in performing. There is no joy in executing. This is why test executors want to get rid of it and go do something else such as, ahem, writing scripts. However, there are testers who "perform" tests and they enjoy doing it and they want to stick to it.

Performing is the most joyful activity in testing for testers. This is a time spent conversing with the product. All other times they are conversing with people. The level of joy depends on how much information they have discovered and how much information they gather to influence stakeholders.

This is also where testers "apply" their learning about the product and customers to see if the product is congruent with the learning they have had.

Heuristics and Oracles

When we discovered these terms in testing through Rapid Software Testing, we felt this was Greek and Latin. When we understood the meaning and how going deeper to learn them enabled us to perform tests and discover more information per performing session, we were ecstatic.

Let us simplify this for you.

Heuristic is an idea that can fail. A test idea that can help us find the answer we are looking for or may not also produce an answer we are looking for. A question that we ask the product. An experiment that can lead us to something or lead us to nothing.

Oracle is the mechanism through which our brain can recognize problems. When we were kids, in a book, we had images of animals and were taught the names of those animals. When we saw the animal in person - we could absolutely say the animal's name. Oracle works the same way. Once testers are exposed to a pattern of possible problems, the mind recognizes it when it is exposed to anything that matches the pattern.

As an example, "Inconsistency within the product" is a powerful Oracle that helps us sensitize if there is any behaviour that is different from the general design and flow. This has an impact on the customers using the product. Steven Krug published a book on design titled, "Don't make me think."

When customers use a product - the more we make them think about how to use the product we are taking them away from the problem they intend to solve using the product. Inconsistency within the product is a powerful oracle that helps us spot patterns that can make our customers think. They aren't coming to the product to think. They will always switch to another product that helps them think less.

In Moolya, as a part of training to be a Moolya Tester, we enable people with Heuristics and Oracles that have been helping people to enjoy (discover) more while performing. The more Heuristics and Oracles testers learn, the more information they discover. Equally, having gathered context and then using Heuristics and Oracles, testers discover more relevant information.

What is the difference between Test Cases and Heuristics Oracles?

This is a common question. We are obliged to answer that. A test case is usually split into

- Things to set up

- Things to do

- Things to look for

Heuristics are (test) ideas that lead to an experiment. As a part of performing the experiment, there needs to be a setup for it anyways. Once the experiment is set up, things to look for are what our brain scans as the product moves from one state to another or from one flow to another.

Test cases, documented, narrow the scope for a tester. Sometimes, this is beneficial, but at most times, it is limiting. One test can reveal 10 bugs. However, if we go looking for just one bug, we may find it at the cost of missing out on 9 others.

Most large enterprise-style testing is heavily scripted, especially, if they have to submit all test documentation for audits to qualify the product. A medical device or software, for instance, needs a heavier scripted approach to test cases. However, that is for audits. Not for finding problems that exist. Leaders in Testing often mistake the submission of documents to audit as the sole purpose of testing. They are oblivious to what they are doing.

We have seen benefits in a combination approach and also doing what the context demands (not to please people through documentation though)

Test Charters

Charters are focus areas. For an over simplification, this is analogous to a "module." Charters help in knowing test coverage. Moolya uses

Test Charters to report coverage and document test ideas (a very shallow way of calling Heuristics and Oracles interchangeably).

Splitting the Test Performing part into multiple Charters helps Leaders and Testers plan their day and coverage. Charters give a broad level overview of a high-level function that Product Owners may be interested to know.

Based on the branches touched, the teams know which charters to execute. The following example shared also has an interesting insight. To achieve the coverage we needed for our customer, there were things that humans had to and then the automation had to. So, it is not an either-or and not even one replaces another. It is putting the humans and the machines to the best of their capabilities.

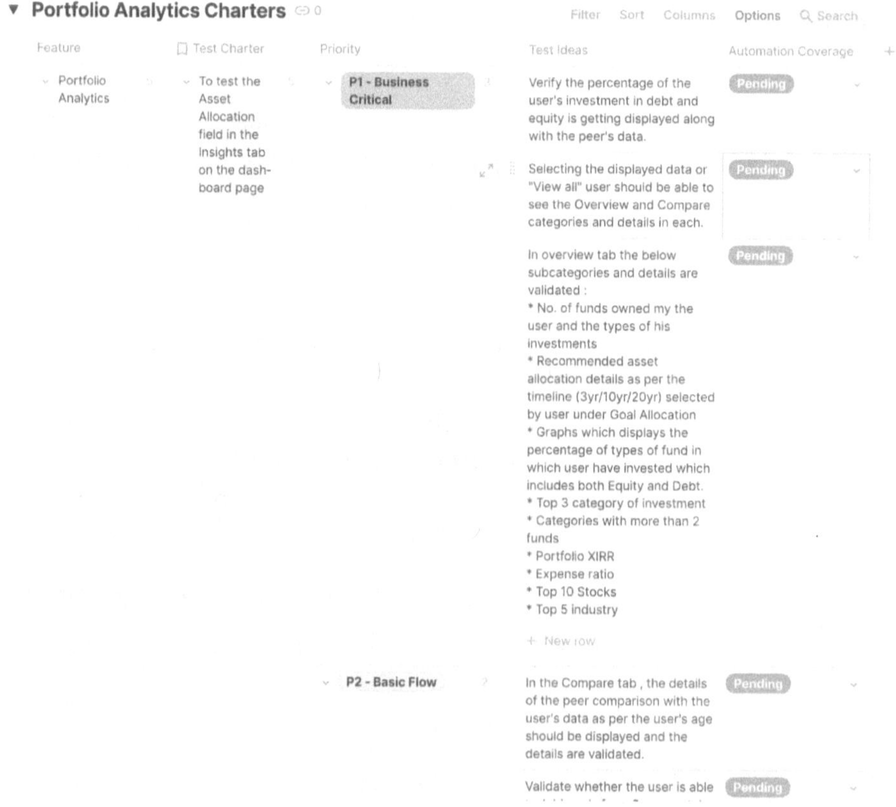

Test Charter for Kuvera: 2020: Team work

Exploratory, Partially Scripted and Heavily Scripted Testing

There are different approaches available to suit different skill sets and contexts. Someone who is trained to be absolutely accountable can perform a freestyle exploratory testing and show coverage. For others, it might be difficult to showcase coverage without heavily scripted test cases. Equally, a system that involves a lot of setup steps to be done before a test can be performed requires a specific scripted approach than a system or a test that doesn't require a lot of setup.

We believe that a tester should be able to switch approaches. In Moolya, we train testers to be highly accountable and for their ability to show coverage irrespective of the approach. Testers in Moolya who have worked across different project contexts have been able to use these different approaches to performing depending on the context within a project or across projects.

Here are some examples of different approaches taken:

User Profile	Visibility of text field and "Send" button upon keypad appearance	Functionality
User Profile	Can I see the skill levels in the My profile screen?	Usability
User Profile	Which screen appears upon tapping back button in My Friends screen?	Usability
User Profile	Tapping "My joined adventures" in More section	Usability
User Profile	Tapping "My created acventures" in More section	Usability
User Profile	Proper message with links created for friend invite	User Experience
User Profile	When getting a profile, Similar UI for all fields as My profile	User Experience

Different forms of partially scripted test ideas in Moolya: Example 1

Premium content features (Article)	Business Week ahead	Pro User	Verify that frequency should be 1 per Week
Premium content features (Article)	Business Week ahead	Pro User	Verify that this section should have text organized in short paragraphs, totalling 600-800 words and a combination for images, charts, tables and text. This will be flash cards visible for a specific time interval

Different forms of partially scripted test ideas in Moolya: Example 2

Summary	Module	Quality Criteria
List hotels for a particular collection & view details	Listings	Functionality
List all amenties in hotel details	Listings	Functionality
List all amenties in hotel details for sold out hotels	Listings	Functionality
Booking a room with the default "OYO Coupon" and "OYO Money"	Coupon	Functionality

Different forms of partially scripted test ideas in Moolya: Example 3

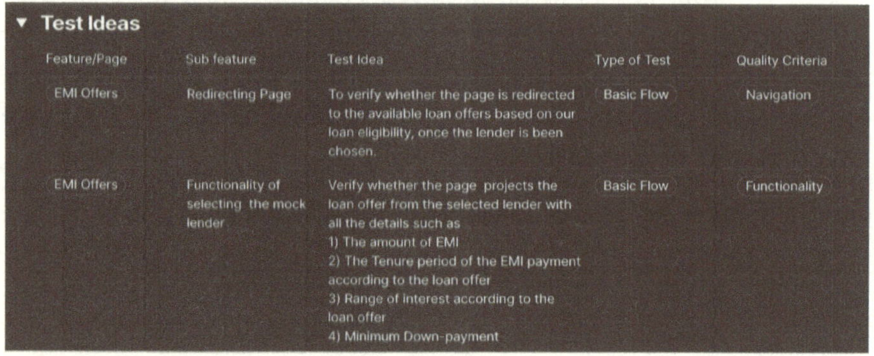

Different forms of partially scripted test ideas in Moolya: Example 4

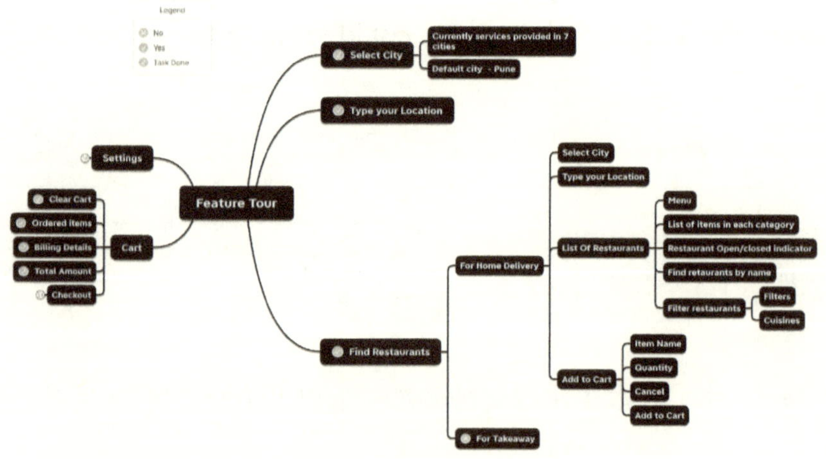

In these different examples, different teams have taken different levels of depth of the script. When working for an enterprise customer, till they are willing to fully believe in our approach, we do a heavily scripted approach too unless audit is one of the requirements we are trying to fulfil.

Skills for performing

The actual "performance" of a test is heavily dependent on the skill of a tester. Irrespective of all this approach we take, different testers do produce different results. Why? Everyone's skills are different. Most testers don't spend time going deep to learn these skills. They pick some of these skills at some level as they gain experience and are influenced by the talent density in the organization coupled with the training, coaching and mentoring we offer to all Moolya testers. This is why we focus on pairing experienced and skilled testers with junior testers or testers who come from backgrounds that expose them to only one kind of approach to performing.

Pairing works great when people work together in person. Some people who choose to work fully remote lose the tacitness and the ability to learn from others. The world is where it is today because enough juniors observed how their seniors (who had made enough mistakes and learnt from them) did certain things. That beautiful opportunity is taken away from the new generation of juniors if we go fully remote. We are going to see a new world with new problems (and new solutions) in the future and we all should embrace it. The hybrid world is better from our experience.

What do we even mean by skills for performing?

Observing

Two testers see the same screen and one spots a bug while the other doesn't. Why? Several reasons. While inattentional blindness can also be a reason, we could always gain some help by learning observation skills coupled with knowledge and practice of using different oracles.

When Pradeep Soundararajan graduated from being an Electronics Engineer to a Software Tester, he thought he could apply a technique used in Cathode Ray Tubes to observing, i.e., Interlaced Scanning. It helps see the screen in a certain way. Practising Interlaced Scanning helps cover the whole screen in a certain way that normally seeing the screen won't. Similarly, there are plenty of techniques and practices that can help anyone develop the skill of observing.

Testers in Moolya are often pointed to Ben Simo's blogs and work to help improve observational skills and increase the knowledge base of oracles. This has helped many testers in Moolya to observe things beyond what they thought was there on the screen.

Ben Simo (https://twitter.com/QualityFrog) often tweets screenshots of problems he encounters and asks, "Is there a problem here?" That's a powerful question.

Hypothesising and Investigating

Many testers get excited that they found something that looks like a problem. In their excitement, they miss a bigger bug that danced in front of them and just left the screen. Systematically training our mind to treat our finding as a hypothesis and building investigation skills help us refute our increased confidence in our conclusions.

When testers find a problem - a high-level set of questions to ask are:

"Is this a problem?"

"Is this THE problem?"

"Is this a symptom of a bigger problem?"

"Will this problem impact something else?"

"Who is this a problem to?"

"Is this problem distracting me from seeing something else?"

"What are my blind spots?"

"What's causing this problem?"

"Is this a front-end problem or a backend problem?"

The set of questions and investigation depth done by testers determine how effective their reporting of the bug is and how influential they actually become to stakeholders.

Reporting

When we built Bugasura.io – a modern-day bug tracker that embraced A.I – there was one thing that surprised us. Our logs indicated bug reports in languages other than English. This means, given a choice, people like to naturally express themselves in the first language. For most people working in IT, English is not their first language but they end up communicating in English.

Another thing that doesn't surprise us is – people who speak good enough English don't necessarily write as well as they speak. This creates a massive drop in what they see - to what they think - to what they want to communicate - to what they actually communicate - to what the audience really understands out of it.

In our career span, we have seen some great bugs being reported as small useless incidents. Of course, also because they lack context of why that bug is critical but equally a poorly reported bug fails to get the attention it deserves. To be part of global and diverse teams, writing and reporting as a skill needs emphasis and focus by individual testers.

Influencing

People who have a QA or Test in their title and can't influence stakeholders are either doing low-value things early in their career or are oblivious to the fact that they are not adding growth value to the organization, and hence, themselves.

Influencing is a big deal. It is, as a matter of fact, the biggest deal in testing. Most of the successful testers we have come across within and outside of Moolya are all influential and they are influential because they are:

- Committed to helping the end customer succeed

- Have built a deep understanding of the customer and user behaviour

- Understand the business needs

- Know the challenges the business is going through

- Prioritize and do only things that really matter

- Not obligated to serve every request coming to them

- Participate in a meeting as an equal to other stakeholders

- Ask fundamental questions

- Built credibility over time

- Escalate things beyond their reporting manager when needed

- Touch areas that have higher business and customer impact

- Had a confident body language

- Their actions indicate empathy and care for the customer

- They hangout with people who truly care for the customer

Most importantly, junior testers think they need to learn a lot more before they can influence. That is not true. There are seniors who don't influence and there are juniors who influence. Influencing doesn't require a title, seniority, a certain number of years of experience, an explicit mention in JD that their job is to influence stakeholders.

Becoming an active paying customer of the product we test

A Moolya tester was part of an early release of an online food ordering app around 2013. This tester decided to order food through the app she was testing on a daily basis to see how the experience is as a customer in production. She documented her experience of 30 days of ordering and presented how the testing they were doing in the company and the customer experience variance was. She also scouted Twitter for people tweeting issues similar to what she faced and provided that additional information to every issue she reported. She also sent specific reports to different departments within the company to help them do better for customers.

Frequency of this or similar or related problem/concern/positive feedback reported. (Pattern Analysis)	Anyone reported the same?
This type of problem is also noticed App store reviews and Google play store reviews.	Yes 5+

This led to this tester becoming influential with business owners as well as product engineering teams. How often do we not use the app we test especially when we test for B2C apps?

The philosophy of becoming a customer of the products we test is also deep within Moolya. B2B or B2C. For instance, we are testing partners with Jupiter and they launched Jupiter Pay Salary accounts. We brought them in as our partners and gave a choice to our fellow Moolyans if they would like to move their salary accounts to Jupiter, and to those who opted, we moved. This gives us an interface both inside out and outside in.

The same goes for many B2C products we test. PhonePe for example. Pradeep Soundararajan makes sure that his first preferred choice to make a payment is always through PhonePe and actively discusses with potential Google Pay users as to what challenges they have in using PhonePe.

For products that aren't the target audience, it is important to eat, sleep, and breathe with customers. For instance, Hilti - a power tools company built a mobile app that they wanted Moolya to help. We weren't their target audience customers. Their customers were people in the construction industry who needed power tools to cut through metal and other materials.

Our testers found a Hilti store 1 KM away from our office and hung out there talking to repeat customers interviewing them as to why they like Hilti. Using this, they derived oracles that helped them catch important things that truly mattered to the customer and none of them were mentioned in the PRD.

Hotstar, a Moolya customer, is one of the largest OTT platforms in India and equally the first one to achieve maximum concurrency India ever witnessed during the Indian Premier League. Most user behaviour is on the move, especially when they are returning from work on phones that are sub 20K. Some of Moolya testers took busy routes across Bangalore in a bus during those times assessing real user problems, buffering, jitter, packet drops and AV sync issues. It was great for everyone to see testers getting out of their comfort zone of testing from one place to testing for real use cases like a real user.

Moto G - 2G(Rel & airtel)
Spice Mi-535 - 3G (Airtel)

	Current location	Start-time	Battery status (Before)	Signal Strength(in dbM)	Video Quality on Move	Battery status (After)	MOS
	Silk Board - Electronic city						
Play Highlights Refresh the score card	Spice : Central Silk Board Moto G : Wipro Gate	Spice : 4:10 Moto G : 4:55	Spice : 42 Moto G: 51	Spice : -69 Moto G : -61	Spice : little buffering. Moto G: Only audio , video freez	Spice : 40 Moto G : 48	Spice : 4 Moto G :
Pause the video and resume Stream the live content	Spice : kudlu Gate Moto G : Singh sandra	Spice : 4:15 Moto G : 5:10	Spice : 40 Moto G : 47	Spice : -69 Moto G : -59	Spice : aftrer resuming from pause, video refresh for time being, and proceeds smoothly Moto G : video did not play and only blank screen observed	Spice : 39 Moto G : 45	Spice : 4 Moto G :
Minimize the app and resume the video	Spice : Infosys gate Moto G : Rupenarahara	Spice : 4:20 Moto G : 5:20	Spice : 39 Moto G : 45	Spice : -91 Moto G: - 65	Spice : Clear Moto G : no video, only audio (A/	Spice : 37 Moto G : 43	Spice : 5 Moto G : 1

Canva needed a testing partner in India and reached out to Moolya. Moolya did a Proof of Concept (POC) for them and what stood out for them in our POC apart from our approach to testing is our proposal was prepared on their platform. So, they saw us put their product to use for sending a proposal out to them.

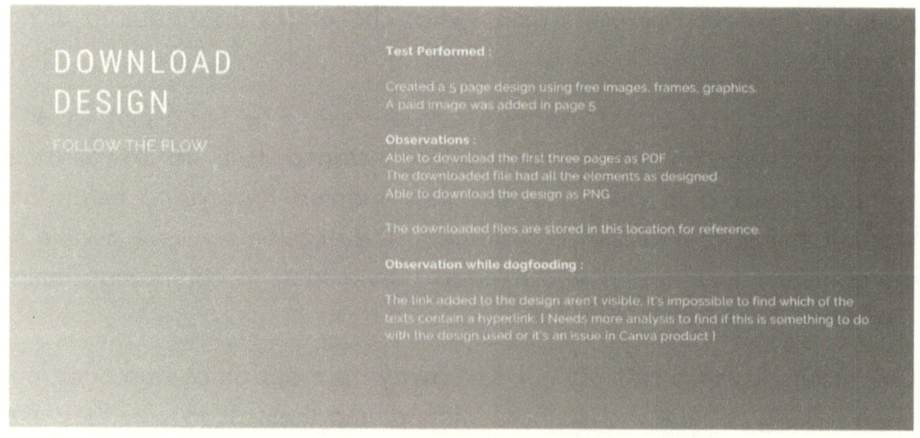

Influence is not an activity; it is a relationship-building activity.

When people who work with us recognize that we live through everything we do, we are passionate about everything we do – they are likely to hear us out. Otherwise, it would be a transaction and no one likes to be in a transaction. We have a relationship with money and a transaction with an ATM machine. We love money and not the ATM machine. That's what the difference is.

Influencing is also not a stage or a phase. It is what we do in everything we do. A simple email we write welcoming someone to a project, a ping on Slack, a bug report we write, a status email we send, a comment we add and even a smile when we walk into the office. People choose to be influenced by someone who is joyful throughout everything they do. Including the way we put our OOO message. That can be influential too.

Every communication to everyone in the project is an opportunity to build deeper relationships. Those who miss this point fall into the trap of looking at every conversation to be work. This drains the juice of life.

Testers without influence are people working very hard and not understanding why their hard work is not paying them off. It won't. The idea is to be contextual, helpful, useful, joyful, and hence, influential.

Training Testers

Critical thinking, observing, communicating and questioning are among a few skills that are hard to teach and time-consuming to learn. The world settles for average. The world has ended up reducing expert testing training to something that is achievable at a mass scale. All that the majority of the world teaches in the name of testing is tools, techniques, processes and methodologies. Most training programs for testers focus on translating a requirement to test cases and running it or automating them. I gave a pause to writing this section and went to LinkedIn to check out the (JD) Job Description for QA and SDET roles. The patterns were pretty clear. JDs were talking about processes, tools, methodologies and types of testing. Not a mention of the impact the role was supposed to deliver and the value to be contributed or mention of critical thinking skills.

Dhanasekar Subramanian and Parimala Hariprasad were among the first in Moolya to build a Moolya style critical thinking training for testers we were hiring. We knew that if we were to deliver this big talk to the world, our training program for testers had to be top-notch. Dhanasekar would get Mobile App Testers started on The Room Game App. The speciality of this app was - people were stuck right at the first step of this game. They had to find clues and use those clues, find keys and use those keys to open doors or chests that had more clues.

This was phenomenal training to lay a foundation for the Moolya Way of Testing in the people we hired. Why? Most of our customers don't have requirement documents. Even if they do, they are outdated. Even if it is not outdated, it needs to be thought through and challenged before it is accepted as a requirement. So, our testers have to operate in an environment where there is no reference but at the same time, the reference does exist in a scattered way, and hence, they need to find them and join them.

The Room Game was a good training ground for people to get used to not having the information they want presented to them upfront. The Room Game was good to season people to be out of their comfort zone and yet give them confidence that they can navigate through uncertainty. The Room Game enabled people to understand that there were clues everywhere only if they knew how to recognise it.

The Room Game was followed up with reading about the architecture of iOS and Android, reading HiG guidelines, App Store Approval Process even before learning anything related to testing. Without understanding how iOS and Android work, claiming to be a tester of mobile apps looked funny to us. We didn't want to create funny testers.

This was followed up by learning our test coverage models such as COP FLUNG GUN, PANC, and OLB. These models became so popular by 2013 that in many conferences that year, either we were invited to speak about it or were mentioned several times. Jeff Fry, Test Engineering Manager at Google, put out a post about it saying he is finding it really useful and is using it at Google. Julian Harty published this in his book on Testing Mobile Applications.

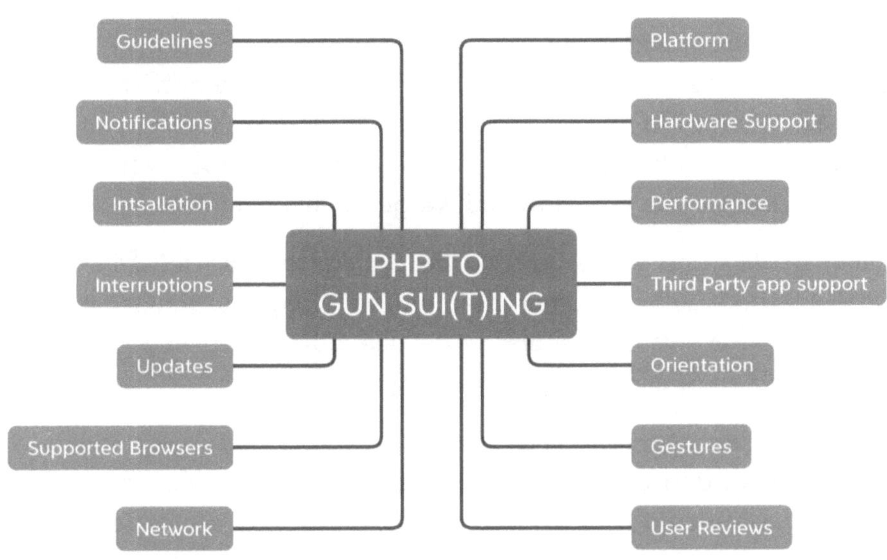

Version 2.0 of COP FLUNG GUN that became PHP GUN SUITING

Coaching testers to test in a growth-driven way

Certain things are great when they are small. As they scale, the quality might drop. For instance, Mavalli Tiffin Rooms is a famous restaurant in Bangalore and has a huge fan following. It serves one of the best breakfasts in town. They never scaled for decades. They just had one centre and everyone would wait for an hour over the weekends in the queue to get in to feast on yummy *dosa, idly vada or chow chow bath*. A decade ago, they decided to set up their branches across the city. Their branches didn't see the crowds that their main centre saw. Their brand name still sells but their branches probably do 1/50th of the foot falls of the main centre. Scaling a good thing is never easy.

This is the challenge every company is trying to solve. Be it in products or services.

Equally, the training companies for talent in the market either create shallow processes following testers or teach them tools without problem-solving skills or making them passionate about testing or becoming obsessed with understanding customers and users. We had to create talent for a need none of our customers and the world didn't know what to ask for. To us, passionate testers, this was the moment like adding a camera to a phone. It changed the world. Our world. For our 200+ customers thus far. How did we get to this point?

Scale, quality and value have to be architected into the DNA of the company and culture. Otherwise, as the company scales, the pain across departments also scales. After the pain hits a tipping point, it results in churn of customers and employees.

As a Founder and founding team of Moolya, we knew that if we personally sat and delivered value, we could do cool things in testing. However, we would limit ourselves to serving just a few customers. We would end up being a niche consulting firm rather than a company that delivered value at a global scale. The value of Moolya should not just be available to an elite set of customers but to every organization that truly cares for its customers and users. That is only possible if the Moolya Way of Testing is broken down into executable forms for people within and outside of Moolya to learn and practice. Many organizations try to fix this problem just with processes.

This book is one of the diverse attempts to enable anyone, within or outside of Moolya, to practice an approach to testing that is growth-driven, deep-thinking, business, product and tech-savvy. This book is partially open-sourcing what we do and how we do, to make it easy for anyone to copy it, if they deem fit. Equally, we share our failures, lessons learnt and the systems and processes we have built to prevent such failures. We are open to sharing more deeper lessons should someone be interested.

We are sharing how we evolved to create talent that was unavailable in the market.

The Kung Fu School of Testing

Around 2012, while Dhanasekar was building the Moolya Way of Testing Training for Mobile App Testers in Moolya, Parimala Hariprasad, who is now part of Google, started building our Academy. The founding team of Moolya that included Parimala Hariprasad and Dhanasekar, inherited training approaches beginning from the Creators of Rapid Software Testing, James Bach and Michael Bolton and experiential training methods derived out of workshops from Jerry Weinberg, Elisabeth Hendrickson, Fiona Charles, Julian Harty, Rob Sabourin, Jonathan Kohl, Ben Simo, Paul Holland and more.

Internally, we called it Baby Shark Tank and The Kung Fu School of Testing and Academy. Depending on our mood that day.

We are referencing an old document here dated March 22, 2013, drafted by Parimala. The following is an excerpt that Parimala had written about why we were doing what we were doing with the Academy after building the Academy for a year. Presenting to you the first page of this document for your reading pleasure.

*_beginning of excerpt_*

What is Moolya Academy?

Moolya Academy[1] is the Kung Fu School of Testing at Moolya. It is the Next Generation Test Lab for germinating skilled software testers. At the Academy, we practice the Art and Science of Software Testing. We spread Moolya Testing Mindset to all Moolyans who join Moolya.

---

1. Plato founded a school called Academy in 387 BC in Athens where he taught Socratic Principles. Aristotle studied there for twenty years before founding his own school, the Lyceum. Academy persisted as one of the highly respected schools for skepticism in those days and nurtured many philosophers who changed the world.

Moolya Academy aims to create the world's best testers by providing hands-on testing practice on real projects to new recruits (including experienced testers) before they get onto paid projects.

Why do we need an Academy?

When Moolya was born, we were just a handful of cool testers from Bangalore. We built our own network with like-minded testers at testing events and conferences and felt good about discovering testers who are as passionate as us. We were still a handful of testers at Moolya who came to change the World of Software Testing.

One question kept bugging us – How do we create such great testers in large numbers? How fast can we create? How efficiently can we bring Warriors into the real world and facilitate great testing practices that are capable of changing the World? (No, we are not talking about best practices here.)

We started asking these questions to ourselves and wondered if there is any Super Talented School of Testing that can provide such great testers to us on a need basis. To our dismay, we didn't find out. This is when we asked ourselves, "Why not create one such great school on our own?" This is how Moolya Academy was born. If you step into Moolya, you'll see Kung Fu Warriors practising the Art of Software Testing every moment with a passion towards mastering it, all this by using their Brahmastra (Brain) and Armory (Approaches, Test Techniques, Tools and Add-ons).

end of excerpt

That was an audacious goal. We needed something more than skills and ambition to succeed in the goal of creating super talent in this world. We needed projects for our testers to practice what they were learning. We needed projects with the freedom to bring in our Moolya way of testing. Not the kind of projects where customers ask us to write and execute test cases or automate test cases already documented.

Startup Test Lab

While we were working with funded startups who understood our value and could also afford our pricing, there were plenty of startups mushrooming and at an early stage. They needed testing but couldn't afford our pricing. We went to pre-funded startups and pitched them an idea that worked. We told them we would bring them a team of testers at the cost of 1 tester. In exchange, they would give us the freedom to test their product the Growth Driven and Moolya way. We also explained to them the Moolya way of testing and more than 3 dozen start-ups gave us a thumbs up.

Tasty Khana: 2013

Tasty Khana was one among the 3 dozen that we worked with when we first launched Startup Test Lab. They were an instant food delivery startup. These were pre-Swiggy days. They needed help and we needed a startup like that at the cusp of rapid scaling and quality at the top of their mind.

Based on their context understanding, we found that this was a high-emotion space. Food is emotional to everyone. We focused on user experience and did an investigation into why there were immediate burning problems and what led them to that point. Based on our context understanding, this is what we delivered to them:

- App and Play Store review analysis and guidance to improve ratings

- Competitor analysis

- User group modelling and device coverage

- Critical set of bugs to fix to improve value to their users

Equally, our junior testers didn't hesitate to talk to TastyKhana users. They picked up their phone and called them or had a chat with them online to understand the experience blockers they were going through.

We laid special emphasis on reporting. I personally hate to see poorly written bug reports. However, as I went back to old reports, I saw junior testers led by an expert tester and coached by our experienced Moolyans who had done a pretty good job on bug reporting.

Here is an example:

12-Aug-13	Cart	Minimum order: Minimum order constraint is applied on the 'Billing Amount' not on the 'Total Amount.' If an item is Rs.140 and the total amount after including taxes is 160 Rs. then also the app gives the message that 'Minimum amount should be 150.'	It could confuse the user about the minimum price constraint as he has Rs.160 in his cart still he is not allowed to checkout.	Usability	Medium

Just observe this beauty

- No steps to reproduce unnecessarily

- Good empathy towards users

- Clarity of the problem

- Straight shoot at what the problem is

- Focus on the impact on the user

- Violation of a logic built by business (hence a real bug)

- Marked it as Medium and not over-excited to say this is critical

This high-quality bug reporting is rare to be found even in many experienced testers. Why? People lack context. When one has no clue of the context, even a critical bug they find - they would just report it as any other bug and move on. The majority of the industry wastes time writing poor bug reports, and hence, testers lack influence on devs, managers and product owners.

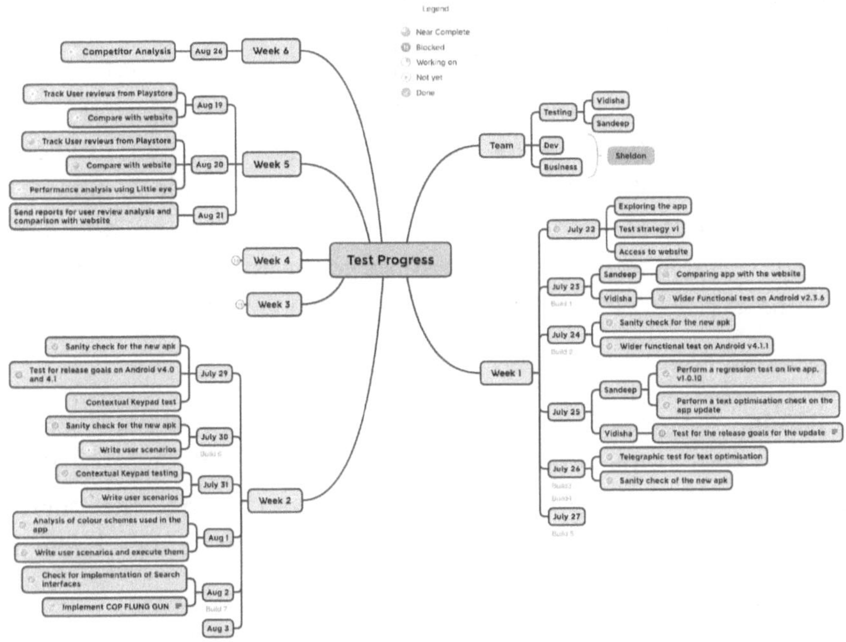

TastyKhana Test Progress Report presented by interns guided by experts: 2013

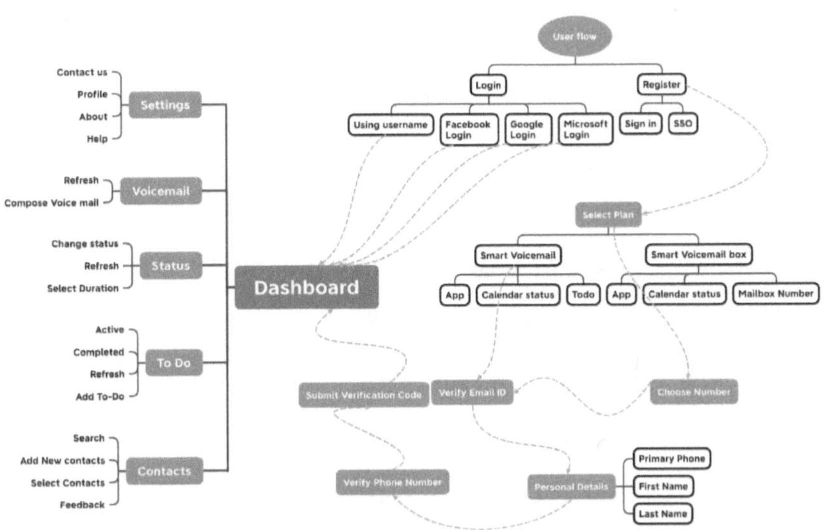

Smartvoice App User Flows Mind Mapping: 2014 by Junior Testers in Moolya

Scaling this value

What we have shared above sounds amazing. It did work for us. It also put pressure to make it work as we were scaling and we also had to focus on cash flows. Early-stage startups don't have cash. Sometimes, they commit to paying and they are unable to afford. We have several tens of thousands of dollars of money that we had to write off because the startups folded down or could not afford to pay after a certain time.

How did we then make it work?

We needed the opportunity to work with early-stage startups badly to create the kind of talent we wanted to create to enable funded startups and enterprises with the vision of growth-driven testing. The only way we could sustain it is to start assessing early-stage startups better than how VCs do sometimes.

We now assess these startups with the following criteria:

- Founders background

- The problem they are solving

- The market for it

- Do they understand partnership?

- Will they pay what they commit to?

- Will they grow with our help?

- Is their ticket size or problem size big enough?

- Can founders sell their products?

- The tech stack they are operating

- The challenges they have

- Are they obsessed with customers?

- Why do they want us?

- Why do we want them?

- What's the future value of this relationship we are about to build for both parties?

- Are they going to succeed in future if not today?

- How is their culture?

Added to this, we have an undocumented ratio of

- For X number of paid customers, how many early-stage startups can we accommodate?

- For X number of growth-driven Moolya way testers we need to create, how many early-stage startups do we need to be on board?

- Our cash flows

All these 3 combined give us an insight into our risk appetite.

This is how we are scaling the model today.

Many startups that we picked before funding, very early stage, pre-revenue have made big today and we are incredibly proud of being part of their early-stage journey and bringing in growth driven approach.

For example,

Practo. One of the most popular apps used by doctors and patients in India and the Middle East. The founders at their very early stage were negotiating for getting one or two testers to test their product because they were super cost-conscious and didn't budget testing costs when we pitched to them. Today, they are a super credible company, one of the successful startups in the healthcare space and have a super credible product and tech team. They went ahead to raise 228 M USD in funding.

Hopscotch. One of the popular picks for baby and kids care products in India. Moolya built their first automation solution and refined their testing practices when they had a 2-member team. They were cost-conscious too during their very early stage and had a very limited budget for automation. We still could accommodate them because they ticked a whole lot of boxes that they would scale and they did. They went ahead to raise over 50 M USD in funding.

Line. Subscription-based revolving credit finance based out of the US. Their founding team had worked with us in the past with one of the failed fintech products. They knew the value growth-driven testing could bring to them and they didn't want to build a test team internally. They wanted Moolya to come in very early while they were bootstrapped. They went ahead to raise 27 M USD.

Today, we can create a million growth-driven testing and automation folks in Moolya to cater to funded startups and fast-moving enterprises. The world today is more ready with plenty of early-stage startups as a feeder to the creation of such talent.

CHAPTER 3

Moolya Way of Automation

Automation - The Moolya Way

What is common sense?

We all think that basic intelligence to understand something is common sense. That, to your surprise, is not the only meaning of common sense. The other meaning is that we have different senses in our body, such as smell, touch, taste, audio and vision. When we see a bottle of water placed in front of us, our ability to pick it up with a certain force is arrived by all these senses coming together at a common understanding of its shape, the surface of the bottle, the pressure one needs to apply to lift it, the possible temperature of the liquid or bottle and when to stop lifting it. This is common sense too.

However, when one mentions "common sense," the meaning most people associate with is the most popular one - to make a judgement or perception that is shared in common by the majority of the world.

The word "test automation" suffers the problem that "common sense" suffers.

The general world's view on Test Automation is – a (or THE) way to speed up test execution (performing). That's a very narrow view of Test Automation

Testing involves:

- Context understanding

- Questioning

89

- Visualizing

- Strategizing

- Setup

- Performing

- Influencing

- Prioritizing based on new information gained

- Altering course based on new information

All of that together is testing. Taking one part of it, which in the case of automation is performing and automating that to call it test automation is narrow tunnel vision. While sufficient has been written about "performing automation," we wanted to focus on a holistic view of automation, and hence, you may not find typical things people talk about in the name of automation in this chapter.

We have built tools, testability, test execution automation frameworks, scripts, utilities and macros that at some level amount to some parts of testing being automated. Having a narrow focus on speed leads to missing other key factors like effectiveness and efficiencies that are not factored into.

When automation is viewed as mimicking human actions at increased speed, it often leads to obsolete frameworks and scripts sitting for some human to touch it to make it work all the time. Imagine the innovators who worked on creating vacuum robots restricted their imagination to mimic how humans clean the floor. Still, they would get an automated solution, but maybe, a human-sized robot with automated arms occupying a large space, expensive to build and hard to maintain. Overall effectiveness compared to the cost would have been negative. Instead, approaching from a clean slate, factoring in effectiveness, efficiency and the factoring in the strengths of robotics, born a robotic vacuum cleaner that accomplishes tasks in its own way, not mimicking a human. Maybe, the reason why the automatic majority of machines to make Indian food failed while the Americans succeeded in mass production and created a whole new standardized fast food industry and scaled.

Moolya's approach to automation is around a similar philosophy. We look at how automation helps achieve our testing goals rather than having automation as the goal.

"Test automation shouldn't be a (testing) goal; test automation helps you achieve (testing) goals." – Jonathan Kohl

Moolya never looks at automation as mimicking manual (*popular common sense word for supposedly human brain activity*) tests but rather looks at what other benefits can be bundled while automating tests. If speed was the only reason, trying to mimic a human hand is never going to help in ROI. Most tests, especially at the UI layer, need more hands to keep fixing the failing script than the hands originally needed to run the test. The amount of time taken to create those tests, test those tests, fix the tests for bugs, retest the tests that test the product, review the code, and execute it is always going to be more than the time required to run those tests 10-20 times of what people thought are replacing.

Mindset: Companies who build automation tools always showcase the ROI of their tool in comparison with the human speed of execution. For over a few decades, leadership at several organizations have repeatedly listened to the pitch of automation in testing as a way to replace what a human is performing. Moolya looks at automation as not the only way to speed but bring in efficiency, and effectiveness while automating. In Moolya, test automation is not automating tests. Moolyans who write code are trained first on the mindset of what automation is rather than training them on popular tools.

Instead, the focus is to make the Moolyans ask questions about the overall effectiveness of automation; not just speed. The training program internally designed to help someone learn to automate starts with understanding and mastering technology. What is supposed to be a shell script shouldn't end up becoming a framework.

Example 1

Automation - API Collections

Test automation doesn't always have to focus on test case automation as we have mentioned before.

Here is an example of creating API collections to make everyone's life easier. In the era of microservices, we end up having too many endpoints to remember. Testers don't need to wait for developers to create API collections and write scripts to test, deploy or configure environments.

Shanmugam, one of the Moolyans, demonstrated this beautifully. He started collating all the API endpoints, as postman collections and created simple sanity checks. Upon completing that, the team found an opportunity to further enhance it to automate test data creation and for environment configurations as well. This helped our testers as well as developers to create different configurations and run sanity checks in their environments, with a simple workflow. This automation even assists BA to quickly prep the environment for any demo to the prospective clients/stakeholders and also to validate and update his approval for the sprint stories.

As a next step, the team automated creating instances. Our customer was using a self-service instance, which has limited validity to control the cloud expense. This means new instances to be created whenever the validity expires. This process was made efficient by creating postman automation scripts that can deploy a new instance or extend the validity or backup and restore an existing instance.

Thus a single tool (Postman) and some basic scripts written, solved the problem of:

- Deploying instances

- Configuring environments

- Creating or restoring bulk data

- Sanity tests

without using fancy complex frameworks.

Example 2

Here is an example of how not focusing on popular testing tools or frameworks but looking at an approach that helps automation to be efficient resulted in using data science libraries like Pandas instead of using a de-facto standard automation framework.

The problem we tried to address in the Wordly project while automating the Web application is to compare two sets of data, one is shown in the application on the User Interface (frontend) for the users to view, and another one is when a user downloads the same data from the download option. There are different ways to achieve this; one is a regular approach of using nested loops, iterating each row, and comparing. This sounds simple but ends up having multiple lines of code and increases the overall execution time of the test suite. Another way would be to sort two lists and compare; however, this approach does not help to understand which set of data did not match, and it becomes difficult to find the mismatch. Hence, we brainstormed further on how this could be achieved optimally, avoiding multiple lines of code, considering the minimal execution time and being able to understand the data mismatch easily, and highlighting the difference between the data sets.

We were already using Robot Framework to automate the application. So, we explored the Python library **Pandas**. Pandas is used to analyze data. It has a fast and efficient DataFrame object with default and customized indexing.

A new library to start off with is a very difficult decision to make. There is a lot of research involved and so many roads to take. The library or the framework can be very helpful for one while looking for an optimal way to solve certain challenges. Pandas library is a reusable chunk of code. It provides fast, expressive, and flexible data structures to easily work with structured (tabular, multidimensional, potentially heterogeneous) and time-series data. Pandas provide extremely streamlined forms of data representation. This helps to analyze and understand data better. Simpler data representation facilitates better results for data science projects. Pandas provide a huge feature set to apply to your data so that you can customize, edit and pivot it according to your own will and desire.

Understanding the capabilities of this library, we could solve the test automation challenge in the project by reading downloaded CSV files from the application, creating Python Pandas DataFrames (a DataFrame is a two-dimensional data structure, i.e., data is aligned in a tabular fashion in rows and columns.), and comparing the Data Frames. By this, we achieved the optimal way we initially looked for, i.e., avoiding multiple lines of code, considering the minimal execution time and being able to understand the data mismatch easily that highlighted the difference between the data sets. This is how we solved the problem by defining a generic method that we could reuse across the project in multiple tests.

Below is a code snippet and the entire code can be downloaded from Moolya Github.

```python
import warnings
warnings.simplefilter(action="ignore", category=FutureWarning)
import shutil
import random
import pandas
import string
import arrow
import numpy



class CreateDataFrame:

    def read_csv_file(self, filePath: str, dataType=str)
->"DataFrameMethods":
        """Read the CSV file and convert it into a DataFrame
        >>> CreateDataFrame().read_csv_file("myData.csv")
        """

        # Check if the given path is valid
        self.validate_file_path(filePath, ".csv")
        # Read the csv file
        self.dataFrame = pandas.read_csv(filePath, dtype=dataType)
        # Return the DataFrameMethods instance for method cascading
        return self.DataFrameMethods(self.dataFrame)


    def read_excel_file(self, filePath: str, sheetName: Union[str, int] = 0,
dataType=str) -> "DataFrameMethods":
        """Read the (xls | xlsx) file and convert it into a DataFrame
        >>> CreateDataFrame().read_excel_file("myData.xlsx", "Sheet1")
        >>> CreateDataFrame().read_excel_file("myData.xlsx", 0)
        """
        # Check if the given path is valid
self.validate_file_path(filePath, (".xlsx", ".xls"))
```

```python
        # Read the excel file
        self.dataFrame = pandas.read_excel(filePath, sheet_
name=sheetName, dtype=dataType)
        # Return the DataFrameMethods instance for method cascading
        return self.DataFrameMethods(self.dataFrame)


    def read_json_file(self, filePath: str, dataType=str) ->
"DataFrameMethods":
        """Read the Json file and convert it into a DataFrame
        >>> CreateDataFrame().read_json_file("myFile.json")
        """
        # Check if the given path is valid
self.validate_file_path(filePath, ".json")
        # Read the json file
        self.dataFrame = pandas.read_json(filePath, orient="records",
dtype=dataType)
        # Return the DataFrameMethods instance for method cascading
        return self.DataFrameMethods(self.dataFrame)


    def read_data_frame(self, dataframe: pandas.DataFrame) ->
"DataFrameMethods":
        """Loads the DataFrame
        >>> CreateDataFrame().read_data_frame(MyDataFrame)
        """
        # Check if the given argument type is dataframe
        if not isinstance(dataframe, pandas.DataFrame):
            raise ValueError("Expected data in DataFrame")
        self.dataFrame = dataframe
        return self.DataFrameMethods(self.dataFrame)


    def convert_to_dataframe(self, data: list[dict], dataType=str) ->
"DataFrameMethods":
        """Covert the list[dict] to the DataFrame
        >>> CreateDataFrame().convert_to_dataframe(MyExpectedData)
        """
        # Check if the given argument type is list
        if not isinstance(data, list):
            raise ValueError("Expected list type data")
        # Convert the given data into a DataFrame
        self.dataFrame = pandas.DataFrame(data, dtype=dataType)
        # Return the DataFrameMethods instance for method cascading
        return self.DataFrameMethods(self.dataFrame)
```

Another example of how automation test visualization helped testers focus on exploratory testing and not waste time on data collection.

Automating Visualization

Capturing and Tabulating 14+ metrics for 2400+ iterations spread across six scenarios across 7 Android versions, four types of networks, and seven audio streaming Android applications pitched itself up as a humongous time-consuming activity. Couple this with executing the actual iterations, analyzing the results of each iteration, and making brief notes of the analysis. Definitely, all of these activities for each iteration or scenario combination meant an enormously increased amount of time for the testers. It was worthwhile for the testers to spend their skills and smartness in designing the scenarios, executing them on the respective devices with AppTim Setup and spending time in understanding the iteration's results, making quick comparisons if required with the previous iterations, and making notes of the analysis, rather than expecting them to tabulate each of the 14 metrics into a Google sheet manually each time.

AppTim offers an HTML report with a decent UI post each iteration's execution. But the reports were not helpful for our needs. AppTim's reports did not offer a summary based on several iterations, say, for one of the scenarios of the Gaana app on one of the network types on a particular OS. This is where Moolya assessed the need to bring in sensible automation to bring down the scenario execution time for our testers by automating the capture and tabulation of 14+ metrics for all of their 2400+ iterations.

All our testers had to do was execute an iteration with AppTim and paste a few of the URLs generated for the respective report, such as the report output's JSON link, and CPUInfo.tsv, Startup_time.tsv URL and HTML public report URL and continue with their other iteration executions. Every 15 minutes, we had a Python script scheduled to run via Jenkins, which scanned through each row of the competitor metric sheet, extracted the available metrics from the relevant URL and wrote the values back into respective cells of the metric sheet.

Scenario	Iteration No.	NW	JSON Link	Android device OS	Memory Max in MB	Memory Avg in MB	Max Heap Dalvik Memory in MB	CPU Max in %	CPU Avg in %
Playing Specific Track in Loop	1	WiFi	link	11	540	345	31	30	3
Playing Specific Track in Loop	2	WiFi	link	11	458	364	29	33	3
Playing Specific Track in Loop	3	WiFi	link	11	509	356	31	37	3
Playing Specific Track in Loop	1	4G	link	11	498	376	33	36	5
Playing Specific Track in Loop	2	4G	link	11	565	400	27	37	8
Playing Specific Track in Loop	3	4G	link	11	511	361	26	34	8

App Script validations were added to the metric sheet further to help the testers periodically validate the various URLs they were pasting on this sheet for correctness in terms of the URL lengths and to avoid duplicates. This way, some human errors are detected and rectified. Here is a screenshot of the app script code snippet. The solutions team has written 185 lines of code to validate the data. As testers update data frequently, this app script helped avoid many human errors. This helped testers to focus more on exploratory testing, test leads and the client is confident in the integrity of the data.

This metric sheet was linked to a thoughtfully designed dashboard on Google Data Studio. The refresh rate for values on the dashboard was

```
function urlCheck() {
  let sheet=SpreadsheetApp.getActiveSpreadsheet();
  let table = sheet.getDataRange();
  let values = table.getValues();
  let index = 1, looper = 0;
  let jsonArr = [];

  while(values[index][3] !== ""){
    jsonArr[looper++] = values[index++][3];
    if(values[index] == undefined)
      break;
  }

  Logger.log(jsonArr);
  const duplicateElements = toFindDuplicates(jsonArr);
  if(duplicateElements.length > 0){
    Logger.log("There are duplicate items and here is the list: " +
duplicateElements );
```

```
      SpreadsheetApp.getUi().alert('Oh No!!', 'There are duplicate items
and here is the list: ' + duplicateElements,
SpreadsheetApp.getUi().ButtonSet.OK);
  }
  else{
    Logger.log("Congrats!! There are no duplicate elements");
    SpreadsheetApp.getUi().alert('Congrats!!', 'There are no duplicate
elements', SpreadsheetApp.getUi().ButtonSet.OK);
  }
}


function toFindDuplicates(arry) {
    const uniqueElements = new Set(arry);
    const filteredElements = arry.filter(item => {
        if (uniqueElements.has(item)) {
            uniqueElements.delete(item);
        } else {
            return item;
        }
    });

    return filteredElements;
}
```

set to 15 minutes. This meant that the metric sheet and the dashboard were in sync. By looking at the dashboard, stakeholders could easily assess the execution progress and the performance metrics comparison.

The visualization (shown in Part 2) is an outcome of a very well-thought-through approach that made use of automation not to execute tests but to visualize and influence the customer. Also, ensuring data integrity.

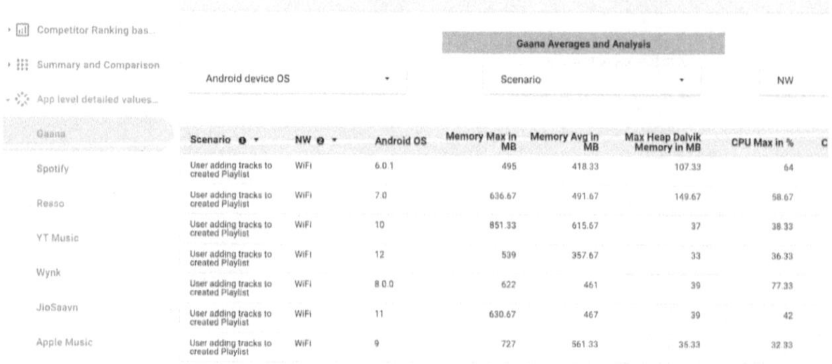

Gaana	Scenario ⓘ ▾	NW ❓ ▾	Android OS	Memory Max in MB	Memory Avg in MB	Max Heap Dalvik Memory in MB	CPU Max in %	C
Spotify	User adding tracks to created Playlist	WiFi	6.0.1	495	418.33	107.33	64	
Reaso	User adding tracks to created Playlist	WiFi	7.0	636.67	491.67	149.67	58.67	
YT Music	User adding tracks to created Playlist	WiFi	10	851.33	615.67	37	38.33	
	User adding tracks to created Playlist	WiFi	12	539	357.67	33	36.33	
Wynk	User adding tracks to created Playlist	WiFi	8.0.0	622	461	39	77.33	
JioSaavn	User adding tracks to created Playlist	WiFi	11	630.67	467	39	42	
Apple Music	User adding tracks to created Playlist	WiFi	9	727	561.33	35.33	32.33	

Automation: Performing

We do automate tests. While we were testing a Flipkart ebook, there was an issue with some books on production. Some books fail to open after purchase. To find these before-use finds, a simple (quick and dirty) script was written just to repeatedly go, buy all new books uploaded on that day (data comes as excel from backend team), download, open and check. This script does nothing other than that, but running this for a few weeks helped to narrow down the pattern of failures, and the issue was fixed once and for all, and we retired the script. This again does not need any heavy investment in the framework, and coding standards, but given the need, a quick and dirty script helped to achieve our testing goal of helping the engineering team to find the failure points.

Moolya testers go through the thinking and acting described in part 2.

Here is an example of a test automation strategy.

Automation: Checks

The popular Test Pyramid suggests that the best automation candidates are the APIs and integration level rather than UI. Isn't it ironic that we create many automated interactions at the User Interface level rather than at the programmatic interface? For one of our enterprise customers who were in the space of clinical trials, there was a need for data validation from DB0 to DB1 to DB2 and to DB7 warehouse and DB2-API. While our customer was exploring a highly-priced commercial tool, our testers on the team decided to attempt a solution using a freely available open-source generic framework and Python. In a few weeks' time, the team was able to crack the validation of the data transfer without spending money on commercial tools. The customer also approved our approach and decided to go ahead with our solution. On top of the Robot framework, our team built custom libraries in Python to automate certain data validation. It has been three years and this solution has continued to be in use by our customer to validate data transfer.

```python
from DatabaseLibrary import DatabaseLibrary
import sys
from robot.api import logger


class DatabaseLibraryExtend(DatabaseLibrary):
    ROBOT_LIBRARY_SCOPE = 'TEST SUITE'


    def query(self, selectStatement, sansTran=False, returnAsDict=False):
        cur = None
        try:
            cur = self._dbconnection.cursor()
            logger.info('Executing : Query  |  %s ' % selectStatement)
            if self.db_api_module_name in ["cx_Oracle"]:
                cur.prefetchrows = 5000
                cur.arraysize = 5000
            self.__execute_sql(cur, selectStatement)
            allRows = cur.fetchall()
            if returnAsDict:
                mappedRows = []
                col_names = [c[0] for c in cur.description]
                for rowIdx in range(len(allRows)):
                    d = {}
                    for colIdx in range(len(allRows[rowIdx])):
                        d[col_names[colIdx]] = allRows[rowIdx][colIdx]
                    mappedRows.append(d)
                return mappedRows
            return allRows
        finally:
            if cur:
                if not sansTran:
                    self._dbconnection.rollback()


    def __execute_sql(self, cur, sqlStatement):
        return cur.execute(sqlStatement)
```

```python
import pandas as pd
import numpy as np
import datetime
from openpyxl import load_workbook
import os



def Parse_Dict_With_Col(master_result_file, study_name, table_name,
list_of_dict, col_list):
    ''' from list_of_dict extracts only columns in col_list and
return those value as a list of set'''
    try:
        to_df = pd.DataFrame(list_of_dict)
        to_df_with_req_col = to_df[col_list].copy()
        records = to_df_with_req_col.to_records(index=False)
        records = list(records)
        print('*DEBUG* ==Records==', records)
        if len(col_list) == 1:
            value = 'magic'
            records = [tuple([value]+list(each)) for each in records]
            print('*DEBUG* ==Records after adding magic==', records)
            return records
        return records
    except Exception as e:
        Result_to_Master(master_result_file=master_result_file,
            study_name=study_name, table_name=table_name, exception=e)


def Prepare_Source_Target_Validate(mapping_rslt, lookup_rslt, target_rslt,
merger_col, data_structure, sort_val, result_dir, diff_csv_dir, table_
name, master_result_file, crf_version, study_name, log_level):
    ''' Gets 3 dicts, convert to df, inner merge first 2 on merger_col, sort
the df, compare it with the third df. If there is a differece, it will put
that to a csv with count, if not exit the function only printing the count'''
    try:
        mapping_df = pd.DataFrame(mapping_rslt)
        lookup_df = pd.DataFrame(lookup_rslt)
        target_df = pd.DataFrame(target_rslt)
        merged_df = pd.merge(left=mapping_df, right=lookup_df, how='left',
left_on=merger_col, right_on=merger_col)
        source_data = merged_df[data_structure]
        source_data = source_data.sort_values(sort_val)
        if log_level == 'DEBUG':
```

```python
            source_data.to_csv('mergeresult_'+table_name+'.csv')
        target_data = target_df[data_structure]
        target_data = target_data.sort_values(sort_val)
        filename = ''
        #Below code for finding difference
        diff_df = pd.concat([[source_data, target_data])
        diff_df = diff_df.reset_index(drop=True)
        diff_df_gpby = diff_df.groupby(list(diff_df.columns))
        idx = [x[0] for x in diff_df_gpby.groups.values() if len(x) == 1]
        diff_df = diff_df.reindex(idx)
        if diff_df.empty:
            result = {"result": "Both source and target matches for table",
"status":"PASS"}
        else:
            filename = table_name+'.csv'
            diff_df = diff_df.sort_values(sort_val)
            if not os.path.exists(diff_csv_dir):
                os.makedirs(diff_csv_dir)
            diff_df.to_csv(diff_csv_dir+filename, index=False)
            result = {"result": "Difference in table found",
"status": "FAIL"}
        len_source = len(source_data.index)
        len_target = len(target_data.index)
        Result_to_Master(master_result_file, crf_version, study_name,
table_name,len_source, len_target, filename)
        return result
    except Exception as e:
        Result_to_Master(master_result_file=master_result_file, crf_
version=crf_version,study_name=study_name, table_name=table_name,
exception=e)
        return {"result": "There is an exception", "exception": e, "status":
"FAIL"}


def append_df_to_excel
(filename,df,sheet_name='Sheet1',startrow=None,truncate_sheet=False,**to_
excel_kwargs):
    ''' except df, prints it to the xlsx file based on the columns. If file
not exists it creates one.
    '''
    if 'engine' in to_excel_kwargs:
        to_excel_kwargs.pop('engine')
    writer = pd.ExcelWriter(filename, engine='openpyxl')
```

```python
    try:
        writer.book = load_workbook(filename)
        if startrow is None and sheet_name in writer.book.sheetnames:
            startrow = writer.book[sheet_name].max_row
        if truncate_sheet and sheet_name in writer.book.sheetnames:
            idx = writer.book.sheetnames.index(sheet_name)
            writer.book.remove(writer.book.worksheets[idx])
            writer.book.create_sheet(sheet_name, idx)
        writer.sheets = {ws.title: ws for ws in writer.book.worksheets}
    except FileNotFoundError:
        pass

    if startrow is None:
        startrow = 0

    df.to_excel(writer, sheet_name, startrow=startrow, columns=['Date', 'CRF
Version', 'Study Name', 'TableName', 'Source Count', 'Target Count', 'File',
'Exception'], **to_excel_kwargs)

    writer.save()




def Result_to_Master(master_result_file, crf_version, study_name, table_name,
len_source=-1, len_target=-1, filename='', exception=''):
    ''' functions calls append_df_to_excel with an exception messagge,
created to handle exceptions.
    '''
    date_time = datetime.datetime.today().strftime('%Y-%m-%d-%H:%M:%S')
    if filename != '':
        exception = 'Data Mismatch in Source and Target'
    if len_source != len_target:
        exception = 'Count Mismatch in Source and Target'
    to_master_result = [{'Date': date_time, 'CRF Version': crf_version,
'Study Name': study_name, 'TableName': table_name,'Source Count': len_source,
'Target Count': len_target, 'File': filename, 'Exception': exception}]


    to_master_result_df = pd.DataFrame(to_master_result)
    append_df_to_excel(master_result_file, to_master_result_df,index=False,
header=None)
```

STEP 2 : Planning Phase

Automation Goals :

- Create a stable automation framework.
- Demonstrate Traceability through reports.
- Provide Consistency in the execution of scripts.

Define the framework:

i. Robot Framework

1. Android - Completed

2. iOS - *To Be Implemented*

ii. Initial setup of robot framework - *Completed*

iii. Setup for Android Studio, Appium and VSCode - *Completed*

iv. Demonstrate framework after automating the scenarios android - *In Progress.*

v. Adding generic keywords for framework - *In Progress*

Script Development:

i. Two scenarios on Withdraw/Repayment on Android App - *Completed*

ii. User stories for developed features for Dashboard, Homepage, Settings - *In Progress*

Execution:

i. Local execution for developed scenarios - *Completed*

ii. Parallel execution for developed scenarios - *To be implemented*

iii. Running the scripts on cloud or real devices - *To be implemented*

iv. Dedicated environment to run automation scripts?

Analysis of failed scripts:

i. Rerun the failed scripts - *To be implemented.*

ii. Analyse, Debug and Fix - *To be implemented.*

iii. *Log defect/issue, if any - To be implemented.*

Reports:

Robot Framework standard reports and metric reports.

i. Execution reports - *Completed*

ii. Execution report to be part of build CI/CD - *To be implemented.*

iii. Automated Emailing of execution report - *To be implemented*

iv. Weekly status reports - *To be implemented.*

The above is the test automation strategy document the team created before beginning the automation projects. Automation goals – some of these came from customers and some were identified by the teams after questioning. Then, the team created the document (visualization). This provided visibility to the team, Moolya and customers where we are with respect to the plan. It's not always necessary to give the number of test cases automated against the number of test cases identified for automation.

A flexible automation development strategy like this prevents many challenges the encounters later – like constraints with framework, code maintainability, etc.

The team chose a more generic framework, like a robot framework rather than popular tightly coupled test automation frameworks. Such choices (generic open-source frameworks) offer more flexibility down the line to solve context-specific problems. It is easier to write custom libraries in the language of our choice and enhance the reports to suit the stakeholders' needs.

Automation: Test Data Creation

Another common pitfall prone to human error is creating test data. This is something that can be automated, and thus, free up the test mind to focus on real thinking tasks. Here is the readme file of one such test data generation repository:

INTRODUCTION

This project aims to build a Complex/Huge Test data set (of all models) from this framework. let's avoid scribble-texting from our keyboard when it comes to generating random test data. Anybody can use this framework to generate Lower<>Higher level complexity. If your Test data creation takes > ample amount of time as Prerequisite, Let us discuss here and try to build a script as a one-time job & see if it saves our lunchtime.

REQUIREMENTS

FOR NOW, This FRAMEWORK requires the following:

- PYTHON3
- Please check the Requirement.txt file for further libraries requirements

CONFIGURATION

- Recommending to use VisualStudio as IDE
- Required VSCode Extensions
  - Python
  - Pylance
  - <..>

MAINTAINERS

- Anybody who wants to contribute.

EXERCISE

- i. Create Excel(.xlsx) file with your desired N(Sheets, Rows, Columns & DataTypes)
  - Usage: For .xlsx File ingestion testing
  - File name: Exercise/create_files/this_excelCreator.py
  - Note: Execution time depends on how huge the user inputs are, (Won't take more than a Coffee break!)
- ii. Create TABLES in any Database with your desired N(Columns & DataTypes)
  - Usage: Provide a valid database connection details at **db_connection_string.json**
  - File name: /Exercise/DB_Ingest/this_database.py

Moolyans can make use of this repository to generate test data and contribute to enhancing this utility. Code sample of the repo

```python
import random
import time
import string
from random_word import RandomWords
import traceback
import logging


def random_value(format, leng): #random_value(string.ascii_lowercase, 8)
    try:
        val = ''.join(random.choices(format, k=leng))
        return val
    except IOError as er:
        print('random_value disrupted: ', er)
        logging.error(traceback.format_exc())


def random_from_list(values:list): #random_value(string.ascii_lowercase, 8)
    try:
        val = random.choice(values)
        return val
    except IOError as er:
        print('random_value disrupted: ', er)
        logging.error(traceback.format_exc())



def random_date(start, end, time_format, prop):
    try:
        stime = time.mktime(time.strptime(start, time_format))
        etime = time.mktime(time.strptime(end, time_format))
        ptime = stime + prop * (etime - stime)
        return time.strftime(time_format, time.localtime(ptime))
    except IOError as er:
        print('random_date disrupted: ', er)
        logging.error(traceback.format_exc())


def create_dict(rowsize, colsize, datatype):
    try:
        dict = {}
        for j in range(0, colsize):
            datType = random.choice(datatype)
            type = datType.lower()
            if 'string' in type:
                s = [random_value(string.ascii_lowercase, 8) for _ in
range(rowsize)]
```

```python
        dict[f'Col_{random_value(string.ascii_uppercase,5)}'] = s

    elif 'int' in type:
        n = [random.randint(0,10000) for _ in range(rowsize)]
        dict[f'Col_{random_value(string.ascii_uppercase,5)}'] = n

    elif 'date' in type:
        frmt = '%Y-%m-%d'
        stime = '1990-01-02'
        etime = '2020-01-02'
        d = [random_date(stime, etime, frmt, random.random())
    for _ in range(rowsize)]
        dict[f'Col_{random_value(string.ascii_uppercase,5)}'] = d
    elif 'float' in type:
        f = [(round(random.uniform(100,1000),3))
for _ in range(rowsize)]
        dict[f'Col_{random_value(string.ascii_uppercase,5)}'] = f
    elif 'boolean' in type:
        bool = [True, False]
        b = [random.choice(bool) for _ in range(rowsize)]
        dict[f'Col_{random_value(string.ascii_uppercase,5)}'] = b
    else:
        s =
RandomWords().get_random_words(includePartOfSpeech="noun,verb",
minLength=5, maxLength=10, sortBy="alpha", limit=rowsize)

        dict[f'Col_{random_value(string.ascii_uppercase,5)}'] = s

    return dict
except IOError as er:
    print('create_dict disrupted: ', er)
    logging.error(traceback.format_exc())
```

Practical challenges to get automation to work

The honey trap for most tech companies is automation. Why? The belief is "Everyone else is doing it and everyone is getting it right."

When we interviewed at least half a dozen QA Managers from Apple as a part of our learning about the industry, they all mentioned that there is automation in place but is never seen as a replacement for human testing. That's what makes Apple to be Apple. No. We are not saying Apple products are all great. Apple doesn't yield to the world and do something because it works for everyone else. Apple leadership believes their products are for humans and hence, human replacement is not what they are looking for in automation. They are certainly looking at automation as a fast dev feedback loop but not confusing it to be a product feedback loop.

However, the idea of building a tech company and having 100% automation is becoming synonymous irrespective of the readiness to build basic automation. To prevent at least our early-stage startup customers from falling into this trap, we built something that helps them assess their readiness.

How? Maturity assessment.

Startup Maturity	Medium
Testing Understanding Maturity	Medium
Development Maturity	High
Design Maturity	High
Dev Size	5 +
QA Size	2 - Automation
Project Manager/Product Owner	-
Documentation Maturity	Medium
Test Process & Execution Maturity	Low

Example assessment of one of our customers who wanted 100% automation

At this early-stage startup, the founders are acting Product Owners. They are eventually going to hire Product Managers who need feedback loops internally. If all testing is automated, PMs get zero feedback loop. Customer Success teams have very delayed feedback loops for PMs. This means by the time they hear a failure, the customer is deciding to drop using their software. This isn't helpful to grow rapidly.

Equally, young QA Engineers who are keen to build a great resume early on in their life won't have the maturity to assess if the organization is ready for it. They would just jump on their leadership even mentioning the word automation in any meeting and use the popular framework combined with their most comfortable programming language.

Of course, they would show some parts of what they were doing by hand now done by a script. Of course. However, maintainability and scale-ability are often not factored. Equally, when most automation engineers are challenged on these parameters, they take it very personally because they feel their existence is being questioned.

Moolya, over time, has learned to focus on aligning stakeholders and not challenging them. We are all here to help the end customer succeed. Aligning people is worth the effort rather than challenging them. Aligning has long-term benefits and challenging has short-term heroism value.

Why do many companies fall into the lack of readiness trap for automation?

Deprioritized Testing Foundation

Even for those who call it "Test Automation," they want to skip the Test part and get to the Automation part. Unless a solid foundation for testing is laid directly jumping to automation screws up any value that can be built through Testing or Automation.

The goal of Moolya is to help our customers succeed with automation and testing. Just that everything we do we do for long-term value. We are not building our resume. We are building value to help our customers grow their customer base.

We build a roadmap of readiness with Testing and Automation and show progress in every step. The customer gains confidence.

Lack of awareness of testability and readiness for automation

One of our customers wanted automation for their test suite done in 2 months. Another company submitted a proposal to complete it in 2 months. We did our assessment and told them it would take 2 months to build the testability into their product for automation to work half as satisfactorily, to begin with.

"We would like to improve our releases with end-to-end automation," said many people who knocked on the door of Moolya.

Q: Do you have test documentation?

A: No

Q: Have you built testability into your product?

A: What's that?

Q: How stable is your product and how often are you adding features?

A: Every release is a feature release.

Q: Do you have unit, integration and API tests in place?

A: No, but we need end-to-end tests at the GUI level automated. Can you?

A prospective customer who felt that our assessment of their automation readiness was incorrect went ahead with building their internal automation team and ended up in the trap we warned them to not fall into. There is no 100% guarantee that we will always be right in our assessment. However, having worked with hundreds of customers, our assessment has a high probability of achieving 90% accuracy.

Unfortunately, in this case, we were not in the 10% bucket. Their end-to-end GUI automation was super flaky and at one point, got tired of maintaining it and gave up. They scrapped 12 months of work and restarted the journey to build tests at code level first. It is great that they did share the story with us. This prospective customer shall never share publicly that this happened. Why? This will prevent talented QA and SDETs from considering them as a prospective employer.

We wish we were in a world of sharing failures and preventing them at least for others. That is the reason this book is filled with our own failure stories too and not just success stories.

CHAPTER 4

Using A.I. to Test & Testing A.I.

Artificial Intelligence has been around for a long time, however, the new age Generative A.I. has made it simple and easy for anyone to use and build new use cases on top of what is made available. This has dramatically changed the world. ProductHunt.com - a great place on the internet to discover new-age products is buzzing with A.I.-based applications and new use cases to solve a plethora of problems.

Co-pilot has dramatically changed how people produce code that works and the speed at which they can. Ever since Github Co-pilot and Generative A.I. (a.k.a Gen A.I.) products have come to use by developers - Stack Overflow usage has dropped significantly.

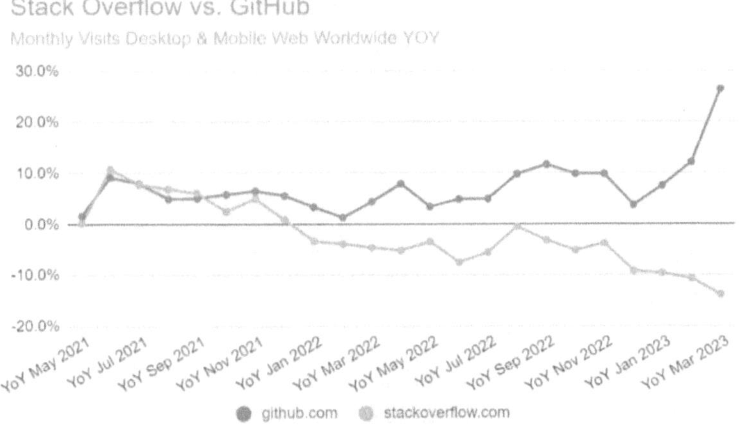

Source: similarweb.com

Developers are great at new technology adoption and anything that improves their focus on writing code. What about testers?

Using A.I. in Test

The quantum of products that are built for developers significantly outnumber those built for people in the test. There is very little innovation that happens in the space of testing. Why? Two main reasons:

Reason 1: From our experience, testers in many organizations are not empowered to bring new tools they like, to put to good use, to improve their productivity. There is a chain of approvals that tires them out.

Reason 2: Testers have a bias to find flaws in early-stage products that make them think the product isn't suitable for them to use and they want the product to have all the features they need to replace their existing behaviour. This makes them averse to using modern early-stage products unless the mandate comes top-down or everyone else in the world is using it and they don't want to be left behind.

However, recognizing these two reasons have helped us build a culture of empowerment of testers in Moolya to try things out and propose new tools and technologies and having open conversation with testers about the adoption of early-stage products. Not just Moolya, there are a good number of organizations that do this, however, enterprise policies and data security concerns prevent a large number of tester population from trying new products out.

Use cases

There are typical use cases and atypical use cases. Typical ones are also shallow ones. People go to Chat GPT and ask, "Generate test cases for …." or, "Python script to automate… " and refine the output to finish off their work. This isn't putting A.I. to the best use. This is replacing Google and Stackoverflow with ChatGPT with an attempt to find a more refined answer, faster. This move won't be life-changing but just a tool change. In Moolya, we are exploring atypical use cases that are transformative in nature.

Impact Assessment

Problem statement: Product Owners struggle to assess business risks based on bugs reported by Testers. Most testers aren't trained in Bug Advocacy and hence aren't good at writing bug reports that are credible for decision makers such as P.Os to act on it.

Solution explored: While building Bugasura (venture of Moolya) - a modern-day bug tracker aimed at helping bugs close faster - we explored the use of A.I. in deriving impact based on the summary of the bug. The first version we released was built on top of ChatGPT and we wrote a cleanup layer on top of it. This gave a generic impact that was only 30% helpful. For instance, for a summary that talks about login issues, the ChatGPT-enabled Impact Assessment would talk about the risk of users not being able to log in.

We knew that this was insufficient but we still put it live to see what value it brings to people. Some testers were really excited about this because using the excuse of this A.I. (that was still in the early stage) they now started to write the impact of the bug on the business, tech and product. This was life-changing. It triggered a thought in them to care more. Most of the other testers found bugs with it (as expected) and didn't want to embrace it. Such testers can never be a part of the team that builds rockets because the version 1 rocket doesn't fly and according to them version 1 needs to fly.

Bugasura A.I. version 2.0 started factoring in the context part and we added a new learnability to this A.I. which was to feed it with requirement documents. The accuracy of the impact improved from 30% to 50%. We saw an improvement but it still fell short of the value we wanted to build for Product Owners.

Bugasura A.I. version 3.0 started to look for similar issues already reported and were considered as P1 for immediate fixes. This was super helpful too because as people type a bug summary - if similar issues pop up - they get an idea of - whether are they reporting a symptom or the problem itself.

We made a list of places where the contextual learning of the A.I. can be improved and came up with the following to add them to our roadmap.

- Customer Support tools - that contain issues and complaints raised by customers and users of the product. This will act very useful to quote the context of the impact a bug has. For example, we want a bug report to contain, "16% of the users are escalating this problem to your customer success teams in the last 30 days" can be the most useful Bug Advocacy with the help of A.I.

- Monitoring and Observability - such as Crashlytics, Sentry, GlitchTip, AppDynamics etc. have useful context about users and their experience with the apps. This can come in very handy to talk about the impact of a bug on production, users and revenue. The day is not too far from Bugasura A.I. adding a line, "Not fixing this bug can cost 600K USD Revenue Loss since this already happened on March 13th, 2022 due to a similar bug that affected Samsung Galaxy users" to a bug report.

Quality Chatbot A.I.

People are gaining confidence in software quality based on tests passed. Many organizations don't retire tests and they continue to gain pseudo confidence based on tests that have become obsolete. We wish someone is working on that problem statement. An A.I. that would assess the value of tests and suggest retiring the tests that are no longer useful. That said, our line of thought is going towards understanding software quality.

With Bugasura A.I., we are laying a foundation for understanding key metrics that enable decision-makers to understand quality and build a chatbot that stakeholders can interact with and ask natural language questions.

Questions that the Quality Chatbot A.I. should be able to answer

- "What are the top 3 things that can go wrong in production given that we are going ahead with releasing this sprint to production with the known bugs?"

- "What tests have we not run in a while?"

- "How is the performance of our application in production as compared to that of competitor X?"

- "What type of bugs caused us maximum revenue loss?"

- "Which feature in our product is highly buggy?"

- "What have our users appreciated the most about our product?"

- "What has been our average time to fix critical bugs?"

While this is still a Work In Progress, we are excited that we are thinking of use cases beyond the typical to bring a profound change to this industry. Moolyans are constantly exposed to this type of thinking that enables them to not just be early adopters but also use these insights to test our customer applications that are A.I. enabled.

Testing A.I.-enabled products

Moolya has been fortunate to continue to work with deep-tech startups for a decade now. Moolya has been involved in testing A.I. products since its inception. During 2012 we were involved in testing a Machine Learning (M.L.) solution built for EdTech space built by Cogknit Semantics. This exposed us to M.L. algorithms and how they actively learn based on user behaviour. In 2012, this was our first exposure to the future that we have arrived at today where products learn and change based on the behaviour of users.

Around 2015, Magic Tiger A.I. - a startup that focused on building an A.I. Chatbot to improve e-commerce conversions, hired us to test their Chatbot and how actively it can be trained to answer questions coming from real consumers.

As time passed by, Moolya got deeply involved in testing A.I. enabled solutions in Healthcare, Retail, Entertainment and Defence projects.

Like A.I., we have had our Learning Time and Data on how to test A.I. applications. This has enabled us to add immense business and tech value to modern-day A.I. products. This foundation has led us to understand how testers can contribute to testing A.I. products

Training Data

Fancy claim alert: A.I. is half as good as the training data fed to it. Many of our customers building A.I. enabled products have one major challenge, to find the answer to the question - is our training data good enough? Unless someone understands customers, users, and real-world use case scenarios, it is difficult for them to build training data that is similar to production data.

Conversenow. AI threw a challenge at us to improve the efficiency of their A.I. and we dealt with it by going deep and understanding their customer context and analytics to build additional training data sets that helped them improve their output accuracy.

Ethics, Bias and Inclusivity

This is such an important topic. People know very little about it but the impact of this on the business is huge. Merely being aware of this does not help. When we look at training datasets or outputs, we constantly scout for issues that can pertain to a certain type of human being misidentified, misrepresented or judged against their gender.

In the history of testing software - no testers up until A.I. came into the forefront of usage, did not think of running tests to identify if the software was discriminating one set of people against another. This requires learning at new levels.

We are working on training programs for testers to help them not just become sensitive to such things but also focus on finding things that are incongruent with the values of the company and humanity in general.

Security

Modern A.I. products will have access to datasets coming from different sources. Sometimes revenue and other times customer private data. This exposes a risk of privacy violations.

(No evidence-backed claim) Hackers are going to be smarter than they were in the A.I. era to build tools using A.I. to violate privacy policies and find exploits and information that they aren't supposed to access.

While Security has been of prime importance throughout - the risk of A.I. systems having direct access to certain information streams makes it even more important. (Speculation) If the occurrence of breaches were x during the pre-Gen A.I. era, the x can grow to 2x in a short period of time.

Specialising in testing for security breaches of A.I. products can now become a niche thing in itself. During the peak of the Web3 era, we have observed a number of people specializing in Blockchain Audits. This was a new specialization that came up that the world prior to the Web3 era had not seen. Many developers pivoted to being Blockchain auditors. The demand was growing phenomenally and there was an acute shortage of Blockchain auditors on the other side.

However, what really matters is to go deep. Shallow learning of security is as good as being aware that it exists. It might come in handy to know but doing it as a dedicated activity needs skills that are built by deep learning on how systems work and possible ways hackers could exploit the architecture.

Business, Customer and User Impact:

Anything we do results in Business Impact. If we lose track of the business impact we are creating, we will end up doing a lot of hard work that makes us think we are super useful but we are becoming useless.

Testing the A.I. for the business, customer and user impact it is expected to create and *not* create matters to a company succeeding with its

A.I. implementation. End users don't care what technology is running in the background. They want their problem to be solved. They are going to switch from one product to another if their problems are not being solved - so while we get excited about testing for security, building datasets or assessing the bias - an eye on the business will make the effort to test a lot more useful.

CHAPTER 5

Moolya Way of Testing for Enterprises

Why do we call them enterprises?

Enterprises are large companies that have figured out their revenue, profitability and growth. They are not in search of market cap expansion, shareholder value growth, market share, acquisitions and maintenance. Unlike startups who are trying to figure out product market fit, growth engines, customer persona, go to market and which geography to go after, they don't do stuff that startups do for a good reason. They have different contexts and different problem statements. The way they make decisions is different and the metrics they focus on are different from what startups do.

Moving from testing for startups to enterprises

When people who started their career in a startup project move to an enterprise project, the first thing they go through is a culture shock. The reverse is also true. The way things happen is different, again, for a good reason.

Here are some differences people have observed:

Startups	Large Enterprises
Decisions can be made bottom-up	Most decisions are top-down
Engineers can pick and choose tools they like	The IT team has to approve of any tool
There is no time for extensive documentation	Documentation is a must for audits
It is okay to fail and learn but iterate fast	Failure is not an option - go slower but don't fail
Verbal and email approvals are good enough	The approval process may have a ticketing system
Open-source tools are okay to use anytime	Tools approved by IT for security only
Flat structure	Hierarchical structure
Culture of Iterative Learning	Culture of cost optimization
Org-level changes are easy and faster	Org-level changes are slow
Everyone has to act like a leader	There are leaders and followers
Processes are few	Process is heavy
Zero audit	Audits are a must
Detailed test cases are not mandated	Detailed Test cases are a must
Customer connect can be direct	Customer connect is via other teams
Code is never frozen	Code freeze for major release is a must
Ad Hoc requirements are welcome	Ad Hoc requirements are rarely welcome
No discussion of test metrics	Heavy focus on pass-fail ratios of test cases
Question asked: How fast are we moving?	Question asked: How efficient are we moving?
Less budget for infrastructure for testing	Large budget for infrastructure for testing
New approaches to testing are welcome	Tried and tested methods only

Startups	Large Enterprises
Less number of stakeholders to convince	Too many stakeholders to convince
The cost of something going wrong is low	The cost of something going wrong is high
The impact of good or bad is seen in the short-term	The impact of good or bad is seen in the long term
Autonomy in decisions	Most decisions need to be approved
Jump in and find out the attitude needed	Figure out 80% before the start needed
Domain knowledge is optional	Domain knowledge is highly preferable
Idea to implementation needs less hops	Idea to implementation needs plenty of hops
Risks are taken with release decisions	Risks have to be mitigated to make releases
No level of gatekeeping	Some level of gatekeeping
CXO's, VP's and Directors available to interact	CXO's, VP's and Directors are not easily accessible
Automation is to fasten the feedback loop	Automation is a way to save cost
Process deviations are tolerable	Process adherence is a must
Evidence for testing is not an issue	Evidence for testing is a must
The time to complete test cases is not measured	Time to complete is highly measured

That said, enterprises are waking up to the startup ways of working because startups have disrupted large enterprise businesses. Equally, there are startup-like teams within enterprises as much as there are enterprise-like teams within some startups.

We believe that the experience of working with both startups and enterprises will enrich a person's ability to learn and appreciate why things are the way they are. This helps build agility and stability in their thought processes.

Moolya way of testing for enterprises

Large enterprises work with other large IT services companies. They don't work with small shops. They love companies with similar DNA. Large IT services companies carry the same DNA as their customers. This DNA is valuable. However, this DNA can be a blocker if the customer wants to pivot their DNA.

Good news! The world is changing. Enterprises are moving to start-up style working and challenging the status quo. The top leaders of a few large enterprise prospective customers we spoke to mentioned, "Cultural shift in product and engineering mindset" as their top challenge.

How does Moolya's way of testing apply to enterprises? Here is how it works. The processes and tools can change. The skill and the operation are still required – be it in startups or enterprises. The Moolya Way of Testing that involves discovering the context, impact and value to be delivered remains the same.

Moolya's approach to testing that involves

- Questioning

- Visualizing

- Strategizing

- Performing

- Influencing

is still required be it in startups or enterprises. Influencing decision makers might be harder in enterprises but that also means one needs to find a different way to influence. Strong leadership in testing is required to navigate through and influence in enterprises. Domain knowledge is a key to building influence on decision-makers.

Building Moolya value for large enterprises

Ultimately, it is human beings, be it in startups or enterprises. The business angles can change but people are people at the end of the day. Everyone wants to have a good experience and everyone wants to build value for their customers. Building partnerships with people in enterprises has always enabled testers to move things as fast as startups. While it may take more time than in startups to get there but once there, things move fast.

The value Moolya delivers is precisely what every customer wants from Moolya. Be it startups or enterprises. We differentiate from the rest of the world in the way we package and report the value we bring in.

For instance, when Moolyans have demonstrated value to such stakeholders in enterprises, the leaders have always opened up their processes to be influenced by Moolyans. However, first came in clear value demonstration and then came in influence.

Moolya approach of testing to core banking testing

Rabobank acquired a group of banks in Indonesia and wanted to integrate all of them into one core banking system and decided to implement Temenos T24. This was the largest core banking transformation project in Indonesia.

Rabobank Context:

- Many people who knew the existing system only spoke Bahasa of Indonesia.

- Adhering to Central Bank of Indonesia regulations

- Customization of T24 to suit the modern needs of banking

- Zero downtime migration for retail and corporate banking customers

- Deep banking domain knowledge

- Deep understanding of T24 software

- Aggressive deadlines

- Project execution on site in Jakarta

- Need for a strong UAT partner

- Build, Operate, and Transfer to the local bankers

Competition context:

- 3 bidders

- 2 of them with deep banking testing experience

- 1 of them with an automation tool specific to banking

- Moolya with a super strong testing approach

How did Moolya win the project among the big competitors?

- Showcasing how we have solved complex problems

- Demonstrating our approach to the leadership team at Rabobank

- Showing how we would use bank employees and turn them into testers

- Showing them how we will train employees of Rabobank Indonesia

- Showcasing a mind map of our understanding of their problem statement

- Showcasing our partners with Core Banking and T24 expertise

- Even while prospecting, we found out stuff that helped them restructure their contract with their implementation partner.

- Showcasing how we plan to mitigate top risks

- Showcasing how we will partner with their vendors and smoothen things out

- Showcasing the list of people who are top-notch testers

- Showcasing the infrastructure for testing

- Showcasing our automation for the right things and not for the sake of doing it

- Showcasing opportunity costs

- Telling them what this project means to us

Value delivered by Moolya to Rabobank

To their bankers

- Trained their BAs and Bankers to become Moolya-style exploratory testers

- Made them self-sufficient to operate with only high-level supervision

- Their own team found super critical bugs during staging

- New UI, UX training

To their customers

- Zero downtime migration

To the leadership of Rabobank

- Successful project completion

- Zero post-production P1 and P2 issues

- Cost optimization

"Moolya delivered everything by building partnerships and causing zero headaches to anyone. The level of ownership is impressive." - Marcel Van Berlo, Head of Program, Rabobank

Moolyans succeeded big way in Rabobank because they were:

- Passionate about making our customers' customer's life easy

- Passionate about testing

- Willing to listen to what others feared

- Willing to share the know-how and make a zero political environment

- Super fast and slow when needed

- A diverse set of skills brought in

- Fast and voluntary acknowledgement of failures and mitigation plan

- Asking for help at the right time

- Building deep partnerships with stakeholders in leadership and on the ground

- Building a culture of "everyone is here to win together"

Moolya's approach to reducing bugs in production for a large retail chain

Tesco partnered with large IT services companies to help them scale their programs. While their internal teams and other large IT service providers were doing the best they could, they had issues in production that were costing them time and money.

They had maxed out on things they could do and needed a lateral thinking approach to testing to find blindspots leading to issues in production. This had to be mitigated across different programs that impacted e-commerce, backend, order management systems, tills, warehouses and storefront systems.

Tesco context

- Production bugs hurting customers, performance, cost and revenue

- Cascading effect of bugs in production

- Transformation to Agile methodology happening across org at the same time

- Everyone including the large IT services doing their best

- Blindspot of why there is an increase of bugs in production

- Stress on teams because of the increase of bugs in production

- Double-checking layers added to build extra safety nets

- Extra safety nets add extra time to get a release to deployment

- Heavy maintenance of large-scale regression test automation

Moolya approach

- Study existing practices across projects

- Run a discovery phase

- Study the bugs leaked to production and internal RCA notes

- Interview stakeholders

- Identify good practices currently done

- Identify practices that are redundant or less value

- Build team outside of sprints to focus on different mission

- Onboard a diverse set of talent whose focus is UX, Functional, Security and Performance

- Re-articulate the problem stakeholders

- Get buy-in to solve problems acknowledged by stakeholders

Value delivered by Moolya to Tesco

- Identified missing testability and worked with devs to add testability to their code

- Built custom tools to complement the good work already done

- Got approvals for necessary things at speeds that surprise Tesco employees

- The focus moved from finding bugs to preventing bugs

- Retired plenty of useless tests

- Mind Mapping training for Tesco employees

- Automation of components that had hardware-software interaction

- Deep connect with business teams and product teams

- A problem was only considered as solved if Business, Product and Engineering acknowledged together.

- Mapping the impact of issues on business teams

- Improved store manager's productivity by 10% with new tools introduced

- Reduced manpower need of 2 teams

- Reskilled their existing Tesco employees in Testing to do exploratory testing

- Visible cost saving of at least 2 Million Pounds per Quarter

Acknowledgement from business teams

Context:

Two teams, one in India and the other in each country within Europe were validating if the rules set per country are met by the Scheduler software. This scheduler is crucial to the productivity of store managers and contract staff.

Before Moolya	After Moolya
India team: 2 weeks	India team: 0 hours
Business teams: 1 day	Business teams: 0 hours
Store Managers: 2 hours	Store managers: 0 hours
Release cycle: 4 weeks	Release cycle: Weekly
Total People involved in validation: 12	Total people involved in validation: 2
Cost: ~40K GBP per month per country	5K GBP per month nett for all countries inclusive
Total cost of all country validation: 40K GBP * 6 countries = 240K GBP per month	5K GBP per month nett for all countries inclusive

From: Rxxxx Rxxxxx, Rxxxx [mailto:Rxxx.RxxxRxx@uk.tesco.com]

To: Kxxx Bxxx; Bxxx Vxxx; Kxxx, Zxxx

Cc: Cxxxx, Mxxxx; Txxxx, Axxx; Sxxx, Cxxx; Lxxx Kxxx; Cxxx, Pxxx; Rxxx Lxxx; Jxxx, Dxxx; Dxxx, Pxxx; Jxxx, Cxxx; Kxxx Lxxx

Subject: Release of Validator Tool

Hi Bxx/Vxxx,

We are happy to release the automated validator tool which will help the business to reduce the time taken in validating all the legal laws.

We are attaching the release notes which describe the details of the bundled package for the tool. The tool is released to Hungary IT so that the IT team can help Business to implement the tool on their local PCs.

We had a trial run of the validator tool on Hungary build PCs with the help of Hungary IT, to mitigate any issues that could be faced.

Benefits –

1. The tool reduces around 4-5 hrs of testing effort from the Business team

2. Efficient and accurate way to validate the rules

3. The tool is user friendly and anyone can generate the tool with minimal help

4. No overhead of integrating the tool with external systems (Dependency is nil)

5. Easy and quick to validate the legal laws for all the stores

6. The tool is not only scalable for short-term temporary solutions but also for long-term permanent solution

From: Bxxx Vxxx [mailto:vxxx@hu.tesco-europe.com]

To: Rxxx Rxxx, Rxxx; Kxx Bxx; Kxxx, Zxxx

Cc: Cxxxx, Mxxxx; Txxxx, Axxx; Sxxx, Cxxx; Lxxx Kxxx; Cxxx, Pxxx; Rxxx Lxxx; Jxxx, Dxxx; Dxxx, Pxxx; Jxxx, Cxxx; Kxxx Lxxx

Subject: RE: Release of Validator Tool

Hi Rxx,

Hungarian business is very happy as we can use this tool.

Our work is much more easy and we can validate our schedule very fast.

I also would like to thank the testing team for preparing the Validator tool.

Regards,

Vxx

When business teams acknowledge the value delivered by a testing team, the credibility they give to testing increases phenomenally. The business teams who saw this value contributed and wanted more tools built to help them save more hours and money.

"We brought in Moolya for lateral thinking ideas on testing and they impacted business, product and tech equally." – Natarajan Alagappan, Head of Testing, Tesco HSC

Chapter 6

Chasing Excellence

Delivery excellence

To be able to prevent bugs for our customers, we recognized that the culture of "prevention" of failures needed to exist within the organization in everything we do to the best of what we can do. This led us to build systems, processes, structures, partners, tools and execution discipline that has prevented many failures before becoming catastrophic.

The idea of building these is to help people detect smoke from becoming into an engine fire. Smokes do happen when running projects for various reasons. A life of firefighting is a drain on life energies. Plenty of people have made a career out of being a firefighter in the IT space. Prevented fires give everyone a better life.

Most companies do have great audacious visions and goals. A disciplined execution is what truly matters to see the vision become reality. Delivery excellence in Moolya was built after experiencing failures. This is how every company that has scaled their quality and not just quantity must have done.

Every company fails but the successful ones...

Every top car manufacturer has had a recall of their cars but what they did after that to prevent the same issue from repeating again matters. Every IT giant has had their apps experience downtime. Everyone fails. The companies who succeed are the one who knows how to prevent majority failures and knows how to prevent the failures that slipped by from repeating again.

Thanks to the long journey Moolya has had, we know 90% of the reasons why we have failed and have built in a disciplined way of learning about future failures and a disciplined way of fixing and preventing them.

Who contributes to failures?

Like how quality is everyone's responsibility, success and prevention of failures is everyone's responsibility. Everyone is responsible for helping us prevent failures and achieve delivery excellence. Including our customers. Our success comes from bringing accountability to everyone. That is also why our customers love us. Huh! It is time to talk about the difference between accountability and blame. Accountability helps people to act. Blame helps people to defend themselves.

Those who conduct accountability meetings prevent failures. Those who conduct blame meetings cause more failures. The culture of our delivery excellence is to help conduct accountability meetings.

Delivery Pulse Check

People on the ground are people with a sharp focus. They are people at a fast pace. They are looking into the windshield and driving fast. Just like Formula 1 drivers. Asking them to look out for the weather, look into engine temperatures, and change strategy based on other drivers' undercutting, is a bad idea. That's not their job. Expecting people on the ground to have a big picture is the mistake many leaders make. We made that mistake too.

Thankfully we learnt to unlearn it and help people succeed. Unlike Formula1 cars which are machines that could be instrumented with sensors to relay back signals to the command center - we as every other company deal with humans.

What would be an instrumentation equivalent to humans? Pulse check. With smartwatches that track how much we move and remind us to move when we have been sitting for long hours, we decided to bring in a platform to help us do pulse checks.

Thanks to Amber from Infeedo implemented by our People team. We built on top of it our Delivery Pulse Check for people on the ground to alert us early on if there is smoke and prevent smoke from becoming an engine failure.

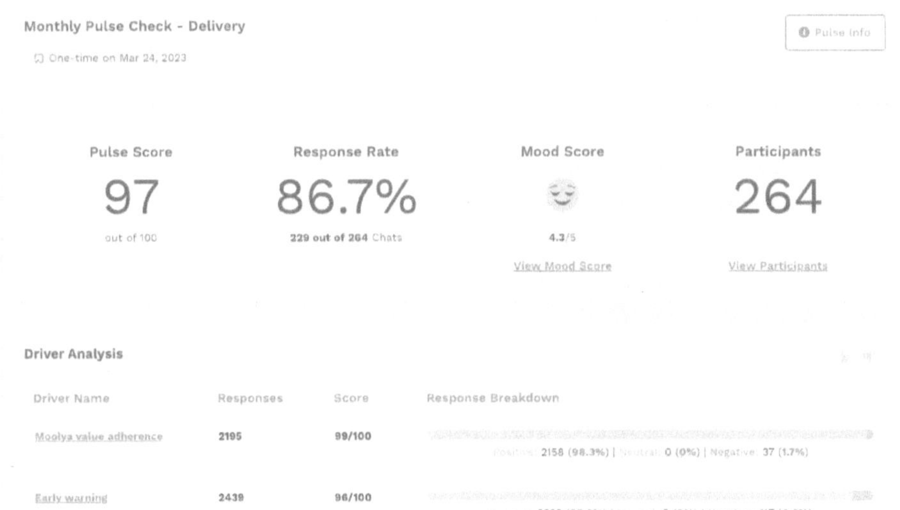

Dashboard from Monthly Delivery Pulse Check

The questions and answers asked to our team on the ground help the core leadership team who has the big picture to intervene quickly when there is smoke detected. For example, one of the questions is, are the product and engineering teams aligned with the customer you are working for?

The answer to this tells us volumes of what to talk to customers about. If only one member of the team feels so and others don't, we know who needs help in our team. We know if this is a person-specific thing to fix or a team-specific thing to fix.

Similar systems exist across Moolya to help detect smoke across different departments and inter-department collaboration. This has enabled Moolya to achieve and demonstrate to its customers – we practice what we sell to them. We deliver what we sell to them.

To our people. Our lovely people. We want them to succeed. We gain no fun in telling them they failed. Their failure is our failure. So, this pulse check helps make most of them to be successful. A great Formula 1 driver needs to be backed up by a great team. We believe in our drivers to have championship material in them and want to do everything from our side to help them win it. This is true for our customers as well.

Governance

Governance is key to our customer's success with us. Moolya takes governance seriously and has built deep thoughtful approaches aligned to the vision of preventing failures and bugs. Like the Delivery Pulse, governance also has a checklist of questions and a pipeline of stages. The only difference is every input needs evidence to back it up.

Blurred image of Mynix.io tool used for governance

Principles of our governance model

- Moolya is an equal partner to customers in helping their customers succeed.

- Moolya and its customers together are solving a problem

- Talking about failures openly is critical to success

- Spot the problem before the customer spots it

- Prepare for the meeting really well

- Drive and make decisions

- Don't fear to escalate any issue

- Don't try to please anyone

- Think long term

- We are in continuous discovery of what is the value for our customers' customers

- Discover context changes coming up

- Ask fundamental questions

- Solve problems objectively

- Offer help and seek help

- Everyone leaves the meeting with confidence and optimism

- Fix culture to fix issues

- People would love to come to the governance meetings again

These principles set a good foundation for us to help our customers succeed with their customers. That's our ultimate goal. All Leads, Managers and Delivery Managers including the PMO teams are trained and aligned towards the governance model and principles to prepare, facilitate, learn and implement the learning and decisions that are taken as a part of governance meetings with customers of Moolya.

Customers' contribution to Testing and Delivery Excellence

We treat customers as equity investors and equal partners in building value. Their contribution to building value has been immense. Every customer we have worked with has had a deep, profound impact on us. They have shaped different aspects of the value chain we have created and are continuing to deliver to all our customers.

Who are our ideal customers? We attract and retain customers who suit our culture, growth mindset, approach to product and engineering and the hunger to grow their customers, revenue and profitability. The mindset and culture of our customers and generally anyone we closely work with has a huge influence on us and our people. Hence, choosing our customers carefully is how we grow our value and is a foundation for making this book possible. Here are a few names whom we would like to highlight for laying an early foundation on different value streams:

Tech, Test & Automation Value

Perze Ababa: Director of QA: NBC Universal: helped us lay an early foundation for implementing a healthy combination of exploratory testing, rapid software testing, context-driven testing, mind mapping and automation. Our first automation framework on Selenium was built around the learning we had working with Perze and his wonderful team.

Natarajan Alagappan: Head of Testing, Tesco HSC: helped us demonstrate the Moolya Way of Testing to impact business and product teams as much as engineering teams. He facilitated us to deliver business and product value by complementing us with what his teams at Tesco were doing. This experience taught us a powerful lesson that only when multiple approaches are combined, the value can be delivered and scaled. This enabled us to look at everyone as our complementary people in the value chain rather than someone being superior or inferior to others. This also helped us build new-age test value for Retail businesses.

Huib Schoots: Principal Consultant: Rabobank: helped us discover the challenges and solutions to scaling the Moolya way of testing to BFSI sectors. Our robust foundation for testing for BFSI began from this experience of helping Rabobank implement a new core banking system end-to-end. This led us to build value for many modern Fintech companies.

Paul Holland: Director of Test Engineering: Medidata: helped us build a scaffolding framework to scale our approach and helped us build large-scale delivery teams aligned with a growth-driven mindset across testing teams. This experience helped us demonstrate the value at a high scale and impact critical releases and software that was extensively used for clinical trials of Covid 19 vaccines. This also helped us lay the foundation to strengthen our value for Healthcare and build frameworks for API and ETL.

Sriram Iyer: VP Engineering: Flipkart: helped us innovate testing apps across multiple languages and build a model of testing that has made us a great choice for customers who want to test their apps locally and internationally.

Product Value

Akriti Mehta: Product Manager: Moneycontrol: helped us build a Product Owner-savvy feedback loop to bridge the gap between test value and product value. She led a one-day workshop for us to identify the needs of Product Owners and Managers that aren't usually met by the Test Teams she has come across in the past and present reports in a way that leads to decisions. This helped us channel our test approaches to Product value.

Ali Masshadi: Lead PM: Medidata: helped us contextualize bug and status reports and make them decision-making-friendly for the Product Owners we worked with. He was a trigger point for us to build a joint workshop between the Product and Test Teams to bring deeper alignment and prevent bugs due to missing or conflicting requirements from happening on other projects we work on. Much later in our life, when building Bugasura A.I., we focused on bringing out the Impact out of a human-written bug report summary focusing on Product value.

Pratyush Prasanna: VP of Products: PayTM: helped us in building a deep analytics-driven approach to testing. He enabled us to deep dive into all user and usage analytics that matter and build tests relevant to how users were using the product. This helped us in building analytics-driven testing and analytics-driven test automation solutions and products.

Rahul Chari: CTO: PhonePe: helped us improve our release readiness testing. His feedback helped us build a robust release readiness criteria for product launches for other customers. He has been a long-term influence on Moolya's approach to testing where he and his team at PhonePe continue to reinvent how software quality is built and give us an opportunity to learn and contribute.

Delivery Value

Sathish KS: CTO: Zeotap: helped us in building a co-ownership delivery that is sustainable and scale-able for organizations. He assesses our value not just based on the testing we do but overall contribution to business growth and how we cater to feedback and fix feedback. This has helped us build similar models of co-ownership delivery models that work for other customers.

Alok Trivedi: Head of Engineering and Quality: Hotstar: helped us build co-ownership models for OTT apps and large-scale teams that co-own and deliver release engineering to the highest quality and performance standards that Hotstar always stands for. Alok equally has rubbed his leadership skills on Moolyans who work with him closely.

Monica Dadwal: Senior Director: Test Engineering: Collibra: helped us with her thought leadership to bring context-driven testing value across Collibra and balanced with automation and governance that upholds high delivery standards. She provides a channelized approach for a vision in testing to translate to reality. Working with her has helped us build scalable large-scale CDT value for other customers.

Nagabhushan Ramappa: Head of Reliability Engineering: Jio Fynd: helped us in building highly tech-savvy teams and instil top-notch reliability engineering practices in them. Delivering mission-critical products with really short release times is always challenging especially when the quality has to be also high. Working with him has enabled our leadership and teams to deliver similar projects at ease and with confidence.

Nakul Moudgil: Director Engineering: Flipkart: enabled in building tech and thought leadership in Moolya. Working with him – many of our people transformed into leaders who today are leading large programs. He was instrumental in creating an environment where people want to push their boundaries, overcome challenges, solve problems and create growth. There is a Nakul's leadership style that these leaders use to lead their teams.

It's phenomenal how many people have made the "Growth Driven Testing" approach possible and how many more have contributed to making Moolya possible. There is a whole new book we can write on how we benefited from working with each customer and how that has enabled us to build deeper value for other customers.

It takes a village, a few generations and culture to build a leader. It has taken us a universe to build us, and hence, we live in gratitude and make gratitude a big part of our culture.

Chapter 7

Servant Leadership

If we consider the population whose title is "Test Lead," the person would have most likely spent a lot of time learning and doing the "Test" part than the "Leading" part. We have met many Test Leads and Test Managers who have very little training or support systems to lead. Usually, such a poor foundation leads to plenty of failures for themselves and for the team. Also, being a "Test Leader" and being a "Test Team Leader" is not the same. People often think Being a Test Lead necessarily means being a Test Team Leader. In some cases, they may have an overlap but not all.

Equally, an expert tester may not be a successful test leader. Most often, organizations make a mistake of promoting those who do well in a job, to a leader, thinking they can now multiply their value. In cricket parlance, Sachin Tendulkar may have been one of the greatest batsmen but could not handle captaincy as Sourav Ganguly did or how MS Dhoni did. This is because the wiring to lead and the wiring to be good at something doesn't overlap in everyone. It does for some people but not all.

To lead is to serve

A lot of people don't get the serving part. Culturally, we are all brought up by glorifying the leadership role as a superior role – one that comes with powers to make certain decisions.

Leadership in Moolya has evolved over the years. Today, there is a deep sense of Servant Leadership and Situational Leadership among the core leadership team and that percolates deep inside the system. How and why did we arrive at this?

Situational Leadership

Around 2017, Robert Sabourin introduced a copy of One Minute Manager – A Situational Approach to Leading Others by Ken Blanchard, Patricia Zigarmi, Drea Zigarmi to Pradeep Soundararajan during one of his consulting visits. Reading this book and reflecting on it paved a foundation for Situational Leadership at Moolya.

This helped us realize that generally, people think there is one style of leadership they have in the arsenal. The Internet and social media have made people think that being a "boss" is a bad thing. People also think that the same style of leadership applies to everyone when it has worked for some. All of this is incorrect.

The foundation of leadership is to help others succeed. It is what others need but don't know to ask sometimes. At different stages of people's careers and the different kinds of problems they encounter, they need a different style of leadership.

Sometimes, a specific person needs a coach, and other times, they need a mentor and once in a while, they need a boss. Most often, they need a very high level of supervision with freedom and accountability. A Situational Leader should build flexibility and diversify the styles of leadership to help their teams succeed. Isn't that easier said than done?

Interestingly, each one of us already have these styles available within us. We have played the role of a coach, a mentor, a guide, and a high-level supervisor at different things in our lives by the virtue of growing up and doing things. It could be at our family functions, our college and school functions. So, what prevents us from being able to bring them to work?

- Lack of context understanding

- Lack of objectivity

- Succumbing to pressure

- Lack of consciousness

- Non-conscious bias

- Pleasing attitude

- Solving only for short-term

- Lack of problem-solving skills

- Lack of structured thinking

- Non-conscious ego

- Feeling validated by the use of power

- Lack of courage to do what is truly required

- Baggage from previous experience

- Fear of failing

- That's how it was always done

- Finding comfort in certainty

- Feeling confident only when in direct control

- Lack of trust

- Believing in one right answer

At Moolya, we keep sensitizing our leaders to be conscious of their actions and what they speak to people. That doesn't mean mistakes don't happen. They do and they are opportunities for the leader to learn. Consciousness is the only way to bring the best leader within us, outside. There have been umpteen number of times our leaders have apologized to their reports when they became conscious of how it could have been perceived. We provide support systems by virtue of how leadership teams deal with escalations, if any, setting examples on how to lead when things don't go well.

Communication

When leaders move from being a supervisor to a hands-on coaches for one of their reports, the reportee can perceive it as being micromanaged. While our intention as a leader is to help them succeed, what our reportees perceive, although not in our full capacity to control, is possible to influence through communication.

An important step to prevent reportees from feeling micromanaged when we switch gears is to communicate and make it transparent as to why we as their leader are switching to hands-on coaching mode. Helping them see that we are together in this journey and not one against another, helps to put their minds at rest.

At the same time, shifting gear from hands-on coaching to high-level supervision can also impact the value reportees can bring in. Any sudden change in leadership style can have the same effect on people. Hence, it is important to communicate the shift and set up cadence of reviews that help all sides be calm.

Holistic focus

All forms of health discussions have become a constant conversation around the leadership team and their reportees. Sports and hobbies are equally discussed. Work is discussed too. A Leader in Moolya doesn't just focus on work but on the holistic growth of themselves and their reportees.

This is not an HR activity. This is a company-wide responsibility. Moolya differentiates itself not just in testing but also in the holistic focus and growth of Moolyans. Leaders in Moolya need to be champions of this holistic growth in life to be able to lead and support their reportees.

Servant Leadership for Senior Leadership

Many people think of the leader as the one who gives out the directions. This is often not true. No single leader is good enough in all areas. A leader is a person who knows when to be led and when to lead. Acknowledging the fact that none of us in Moolya are going to know everything, we practice servant leadership.

Pradeep Soundararajan's email signature says the following:

Chief Servant to Employees and Customers | Founder CEO

Most internal communications have Pradeep Soundararajan being addressed as a Chief Servant and not the CEO. Our titles are for the external world. Not internally. Internally, as leaders, we are serving people who are serving customers and, in turn, their customers. Our Moolyans are customers too.

There are a number of areas where the leadership team guides the Chief Servant to do certain things. There are areas where his guidance is sought too. This is a sign of a healthy team where everyone is equal. No one person is treated as a superior.

Combining this with Situational Leadership has been a highly successful approach for the leadership teams to succeed. Moolya has seen the least attrition with growth teams. Even in Delivery teams, leaders who practice Situational Leadership and Servant Leadership with a Holistic focus on team's growth deliver the least attrition and beat all industry benchmarks.

Our customers love us not just because our testing provides a different good business, product and tech value to them, but also because we have less attrition.

At times, Moolya has been asked how do we do it. Our answer has been simple and straightforward. It is the understanding and culture that drives us to deliver this stellar value.

Principles the leadership team of Moolya lives by:

- People stay in a place they co-own

- Co-ownership aids long-term thinking

- People do well when they are trusted

- A safe place to fail and learn is a great place to learn

- Good people are harder to earn than money

- Squeezing people to achieve success isn't one

- Empathy should not be taken advantage of

- Learning how our customers earn money is critical

- The goal of life is not to work but to live life

- Overdoing harms projects and people

- Passion is okay but obsession is not okay

- Take joy from work to home, not stress

- Titles do not make people a leader

- Enabling others to succeed is how we succeed

- Growth is not a zero-sum game

Failure case studies

Companies usually document their success as case studies. We think it is important to document failure case studies. They are a key source of learning for everyone in the org. Unfortunately, when failures are not discussed openly, the next generation of leaders repeat the same mistakes and go through the same set of learning. However, that is not progress. That is people falling into lower levels of loops of growth.

In every town hall, we built a culture of discussing red flags and failures. This culture does a couple of things. People see that failure is being openly discussed and that people are not being punished for failure. This opens people up to be free and not constrained or worried about consequences. This is a big confidence booster for many. We still live in a world where people don't make their own career decisions. They look for the world around them to validate their career decisions. Generally, people are poor decision-makers because they don't want to be alone in failure. Such people can never grow as leaders by example. Maybe by title only.

Failure Case study 1: Losing sight of purpose

A customer who is a leader in the OTT space reached out to us having listened to the success story we created for other OTT players.

Who reached out to us and why?

Context matters in Moolya. The leadership team at the customer location realized that their existing test team had been doing good but no new thoughts were coming. They wanted Moolya to complement their existing team but not do what the existing team was doing.

This was scoped out well, and we did a high-level proposal and submitted a plan on how we can transform their testing and value to their customers. We had a handshake and a commercial agreement was drafted. The engagement was off to a good start.

We built a team and moved one of our leaders who was available to lead this engagement on behalf of Moolya. The leader took over and the engagement was going smoothly. Some feedback came in and we did some course corrections. The client seemed happy with the course corrections.

Although, for us, pleasing customers is not what we do. We serve their customers so any course corrections that help our customers add value to their customers is good for all of us. Months passed by; we hit a roadblock. A red flag was raised by the leadership team that Moolya was not bringing in the value they thought we would.

When we get a red flag, we don't panic. We don't press the panic button. We don't call our leaders or people and start abusing them as to why we got there. That is what organizations who don't know how to solve problems do. As a leadership team, we are super confident that we can solve any problem that is within our realm of expertise.

We did a Root Cause Analysis and found an interesting thing that happened on the ground. While the vision of our customer's leadership team was that we would bring in complementary thinking, their reportees who were execution leaders wanted more hands to speed up their testing. So, our people were dragged into doing things as a support to their internal teams. For our testers, that was work too. So, they got carried away with it. Our leader who should have sensed that shift failed to. Why? Things crept in slowly and steadily. The purpose had failed although we did a lot of hard work and did some decent work on supporting.

If the purpose of why we are there fails, no matter how great a work we do, we have done wrong work.

Course correction:

As a leadership team, we acknowledged that the value had not been delivered. We gave our customer options to fire us if required and a course correction plan if they did not plan to fire us. They wanted to continue with Moolya but with the course correction.

One of our senior leadership team members personally mentored and coached the leaders over the next few months to bring in the change. This enabled them to see the value they were looking for and continue working with us. For the leaders, it was a good reminder that, in the name of work, we may be off our route and destination.

As Moolya we did not impact their appraisal, hike or punish anyone for this. We just brought in the support to help them and make them conscious of such stuff.

However, if this leader repeats similar stuff, we will let this leader go. That is the best thing to do because making a mistake is okay. Repeating it is dangerous for everyone on their boat. That shows a failure to learn and an attitude to put others at risk. We think everyone appreciates this in Moolya.

What are your lessons learned from this case study?

Failure case study 2: Delayed escalation

Moolya has in rare cases let go of paying customers when there is a toxic culture on the customer side. However, our first approach is to not let go. Be it with our own employees or customers. It is easy to make such a decision but that isn't good to build leaders. Both internally and externally.

We know how hard it is to build a good culture in an organization. While there is good culture, every 30 new people that are on board, test or bring a small shift to the culture. The leader's responsibility in the organization is to continue to bring the culture back to how the organization should function as envisioned.

We were working with a customer who was building platforms for large agencies to organize their unorganized internal processes. This customer was well-funded and had been making good progress in terms of their customer additions. We enjoyed a good few years with them and then a context change happened. Our customer went through a reorg that led to some operational leaders leaving and a new set of leaders being appointed.

Leadership change isn't new to us. With the customers we have worked with long enough, we have seen at least 5 leadership changes and constantly sought the vision of each leadership team to align with their vision.

However, with this customer, the new set of leaders who came in brought in a lot of baggage of distrust from the previous organization they were involved in. This put everyone on the project, including their own employees, to defend their work. When people are focused on defending their work, their full-time work becomes defending and not working.

Our leader was hoping that things would settle down but it only got worse. When people are defending themselves in an environment that distrusts them, they tend to overwork. This leads to mistakes. It is a vicious cycle. This started to cause fatigue in people.

Moolya's governance model today incorporates escalations from Moolya to customers. Not one way – from customer to Moolya. Both parties are working towards the same goal and they should escalate issues that need fixing. Escalation is a key skill when working on a large project.

While our leader did bring this up in governance meetings, our leader failed to escalate it. The leader thought they could handle it at their counterpart level. We don't want to offend anyone. Sadly, this attitude puts a hole in the boat.

Everyone on the project was frustrated about the situation and attrition issues began on our customer-employee side. Every 3 months, there were new people replacing existing ones. This led to poor-quality software and blame games.

Course correction:

One day, a frustrated tester of Moolya decided to escalate this to the Moolya core leadership team. We, as a culture, didn't put our leader in defence but did an objective RCA. We understood that this leader had done a wonderful job with the only exception of escalating the cultural issues to the C level of our customer. However, post the RCA, the first thing we did was to escalate this to the COO of our customer.

The COO was absolutely interested to acknowledge and solve problems. He brought in good leadership and wisdom to address this calmly and directed people to speak objectively and move things. From Moolya side, we rotated a few people but kept the leader on to the project. Why?

The leader had learnt a powerful lesson that escalating and getting an issue resolved at the right time matters. This leader did exceptionally well thereafter and continues to lead projects in Moolya. Escalates on time, to the right people.

CHAPTER 8

Culture that Transforms People

History: 2010 to 2015

Pradeep Soundararajan, the Founder of Moolya, built and screwed up the culture of Moolya during the initial years of Moolya. What? Really? Oh, absolutely yes. Every first-time Founder is clueless about what culture is. Until they screw it up and the screw-up starts affecting the startup they care so much about.

Moolya's initial years had a very intolerant culture. Intolerant towards poor quality. Intolerant towards non-passion towards testing. Intolerant towards low-value test thinking. Intolerant towards pleasing attitude. Intolerant towards lack of customer obsession. Intolerant towards repeating mistakes. Intolerant towards lack of questioning. Intolerant towards poor documentation, emails, and reporting skills. All this led to Moolya's customers seeing great value. Our work would obviously stand out. This looks great on paper. It indeed was great when we were a small company of 30 people. Had we chosen to remain a 30-member company, there was no need to change the culture.

To build a large organization, it is important to help B players graduate to A players. Every A player was a B player someday. Moolya's culture during this period was not scalable because it was only suited to building individual contributing A players. While great teamwork did happen during this period it had conflicts unless silos were created.

Pradeep played the role of the guardian of the culture and would make decisions to let go of people who showed a slight tinge of deviation from the A player team he envisioned. The ones who remained in Moolya were all A players. These players felt elite. Moolya had zero attrition issues.

The flaw with this was high levels of intolerance and judgment against people became the culture. Everyone tried copying the way Pradeep was intolerant towards everything he looked at. This came and hit the business because nothing moved unless all the intolerant people were convinced of something. That is when Pradeep woke up from it and said, "I am wrong. I need to fix it."

Instead of defending what he did was right, he acknowledged that he was wrong and decided to learn how to build a culture and started to bring change from within himself. The modern-day Moolya is a good reflection of how the culture has transformed through Pradeep's personal transformation.

Dhanasekar, the founding member of Moolya, quit Moolya due to cultural differences that arose during this period and rejoined Moolya after he witnessed the cultural transformation from outside. This is a great testament that when a leader is willing to acknowledge the mistake and fix it, people always come in and support. It is fascinating that they are writing this book together.

Since 2016

When Moolya culture was re-invented, the need to document it and be used as a reference document was also born. Before the principles of the culture were drafted, a preamble was drafted. A preamble to capture the background of why certain principles are a culture of Moolya.

Preamble

Understanding humans

- Culture is the way people behave
- Most people are good people at heart

- Most people behave well when things are going fine

- Some people are bossy because they think showing off is the way to get work done

- Some people are lazy, and hence, push the good people out of their comfort zone

- Some people are less skilled than others and the highly skilled people can think badly of the less skilled and create friction

- Some people are biased towards religion, politics, caste and languages that create groups and friction within them

- Some people promote hatred towards colleagues and employers because they think something unfair is happening to them

- Some people are interested in gossip and rumours

- They just don't know how their behaviour impacts people

- All humans are emotional

- If someone is pushed to defend themselves, they will attack and that attack can be more powerful than the attack on them

- Their past behaviour is tacitly learnt at home/school/college/ friends circle/ex-employers culture.

- We can't change people; only they themselves can

- Most people are willing to change if they see positives in changing

- Punishing people doesn't help

- Workplaces can have a huge influence on their behaviour

- Money can cause greed and greed can cause a good human to behave badly

- Power to good people is what the world needs

- Hierarchy in an organization is for decision-making and not a hierarchy of ego or power over everything in the company

- Good people with a not so good behaviour need a chance to correct themselves

- If anyone fails to correct themselves, they are a threat to themselves too (and hence, others)

- Most people don't know how to treat themselves well – they only know how to punish themselves if they do something that is wrong

- Most people want to do great work and most of them don't know what great means

- People are usually not wrong with their intent; they are wrong in their execution

- Working with people means working with the culture and hence, their behaviour (not just their skills)

- A Highly skilled person with bad behaviour is useless

- Young people are quick to conclude

- All people make many emotional decisions

- People take feedback as a negative thing and think someone who gave feedback hurt them.

- People build stories of being a victim that helps them get support

- People who end up disliking someone will put in the bias and think every action of the person has a reason towards them

- Insecurity in people is the biggest enemy to creating a good culture

- Anyone who wants to do great has to do with energy

- Energy does not mean they are always talking or roaming around and being visible

- Every person brings a different culture into the company

Context of culture

- We are a people company as much as a value-driven testing company

- Our people are our strength

- Our people's behaviour drives the confidence towards Moolya

- Moolya is not just a place where someone becomes a skilled tester but also a good-behaving human being

- If people behave good to each other, they create an environment for talent to grow. That's the way Moolya wants to grow talent

- An environment where people fight against each other to win is toxic and Moolya is a place where people should learn to collaborate and help each other succeed

- Moolya is a place where people learn more good behaviour and hopefully spread the good behaviour at home and other places they mingle and thereby, creating a beautiful world around them

- Culture is not a fun activity although having fun is a part of our culture

- People can have any kind of fun as long as it does not impact the rest of the people/team/company.

- Delivery is a pressure job by default; getting frustrated and making decisions will do short-term fix and long-term loss

"Clarity is the mother of intelligence" - Sramana Mitra

Any company that grows the number of people is subjected to the above. Irrespective of the country, size, funding, money in the bank, or any other factor. Humans are humans the world over. They have their fears and insecurities. They have their strengths and weaknesses. They are emotional and intelligent at the same time.

Knowing all this about humans helps build a culture to enables them to do 3 things:

1. Succeed at work

2. Have a calm, peaceful way of resolving conflicts and issues

3. Enable them to help each other succeed

Cultural values of a Moolyan

Politeness	A Moolyan has to be polite in all communication with colleagues and customers.
Calmness	A Moolyan should have a calm approach to solving a problem.
Appreciation	A Moolyan should always appreciate the little good things that their colleagues and customers do.
Courage	A Moolyan should have the courage to stand up and speak their findings.
Clarity	A Moolyan should have clarity in communication and presenting anything to colleagues and customers.
Energy	A Moolyan should be passionate and demonstrate it by bringing in energy to the project.
Presentability	A Moolyan should present themselves as approachable, clean, and dressed well.
Discipline	A Moolyan should be disciplined in doing what they have committed to or is required.
Problem-Solving	A Moolyan looks at solving the problem and not growing the argument.
Healthy	A Moolyan should exercise regularly and practice for mental health.

Healthy, why?

Up until 2022, we did not have "healthy" added in there. While we focused a lot on health during the pandemic, post that, everyone started to lose focus on it. Moolya's vision of holistic growth is only possible when Moolyans look at their own health as a factor of growth. Unless we take it seriously and make it a part of our cultural values, talking about holistic value appears to be a cool thing that no one really benefits from.

The world already has enough people in their 20s, 30s and 40s with a number of physical and mental health issues. Moolya shouldn't be contributing to increasing that but should decrease in small fractions.

Companies usually give people money in exchange for their work. This is how capitalism works. Nothing wrong. However, Moolya is focused on balanced capitalism. We want to help our people become healthy and disciplined.

It is mandatory in Moolya to do some form of workout, exercise, yoga or meditation for the body and mind on a regular basis. From 2023, a platform will track if people are being consistent and help those who are not consistent become consistent. Those who fail despite the help provided shall be supported to find a higher paying job that doesn't care about how healthy or sick they become as long as they meet deadlines.

Politeness, why?

One of the differences between civilized and uncivilized is politeness. When we call ourselves "professional" at something, we also mean we are civilized. Emotions fly high when people are given feedback or told they aren't doing as good as they assume to be. When emotions and egos are touched, people become defensive and offensive.

People want to prove to someone that they are correct. During this process or post-proving, they end up sounding impolite. They are right in what they did but unfortunately, wrong in the approach. The net result is their own credibility loss.

Our Founder CEO, Pradeep Soundararajan, had a free flow of using the "F" word for many things during the initial years. He was well respected in the industry back then too for his views and opinions and he was right when he said, "This is too effing bad" but unfortunately, his approach of saying it was impolite. He was possibly a good tester but a bad cultural misfit to any company. Sometimes, people got offended and sometimes, people did not but instead emulated what he said and did and hence spread a poor culture.

Since 2015, Pradeep Soundararajan understood politeness and influenced 10x more people than he ever did in the previous decade. Ever since he discovered that politeness wins in the long run, it has become an integral part of Moolya culture.

It is hard to be polite when going through a feeling of being victimized or bullied by someone. There's a polite way to say, "Leave the room." As one of the greatest musicians of our time, A.R. Rahman said, "There's always been a choice in front of me to love or hate. I chose love every single time and that is what has led me to be here today."

Another Music Maestro, Illayaraja, who may have composed more brilliant pieces than AR Rahman has done so far, made some harsh statements about people in public and that led to his credibility loss.

Talent wins. Yes. However, politeness wins beyond what talent can imagine to win.

Testing and being part of growth teams is a hard job. We will be often tested, put in a situation where we are feeling cornered, feel helpless, feel voiceless, feel offended, and questioned about why we missed certain things by people who don't understand our work but are in a position of power but if that makes us lose our polite nature, we are becoming animals. We may win an argument but as an animal and not as a human being.

Courage, why?

"The most important skill for a tester is courage" - Jerry Weinberg

Ever wondered why one of the smartest humans that walked this planet said this? That is because Jerry, having seen many testers, consultants and professionals across different functions, observed what makes them useful to the world.

The way we are all brought up is by being "fear induced." Once fear sets in, we then hold on to what we have and defeat the purpose of why we were hired in the first place. We fear losing a job, a hike or a promotion. Most importantly, we fear being wrong, being scolded in public, being stupid in front of our colleagues or being impolite to our seniors or colleagues.

Wanting to look good is the biggest reason why many people are not courageous. That said, we must bring in a key difference to how people understand courage. Often, people think of it as valour.

Courage is the ability to do or speak what is right and be open to correction if discovered wrong. Valour is the ability to fight in a dangerous situation. Most often, people suppress their courage and it bursts out as valour within them. That is their fault.

Courage is as simple as saying, "I don't think this is working for us."

Valor is, "For over a year, I have been asked to do wrong things and I want justice now."

Who makes their life easy at workplaces is people with courage. Most often, people who suppress and create a need to bring their valour out - create a dangerous situation for themselves when early courage could have helped prevent the stress build-up.

In a testing context, while we are not gatekeepers, calling out what is a real blocker or what can cause impact to decision-makers and escalating issues when they are not getting the proper focus is courage. Most talented people in testing become useless to organizations when they don't focus on the impact of bugs or issues that can potentially cause damage to revenue, customers or data.

It takes courage to say No. For most people who are systematically trained since childhood to say Yes and punished for saying No, it becomes hard for them to muster the courage to say No. Courage makes life easy. Why create unnecessary hardness in life?

In cases where someone is being abused sexually, being harassed, or being shamed, early courage helps mitigate the issue from turning into a disaster.

Moolya encourages people to be courageous to make their own lives easy. Otherwise, stress build-up bursts out as valour and in valour there is damage, collateral damage and baggage created for a lifetime.

Energy, why?

Energy is the continuous and sustained excitement we bring to do things and take it to completion. Energy is the commitment we bring to doing things and taking it to completion.

Energy is the invisible factor for someone to build persistence.

A lot of people do start a lot of initiatives. Most of them don't see a completion. Why?

Most people lack energy after the first excitement dies down. Only those who have the energy to sustain the excitement beyond the first valley of death are people who are going to take things to completion and win.

This book was an initiative. At least 3 times, the authors got distracted with things coming their way that looked more important than finishing this book. If this book is in your hands today, it is because the authors did commit to the energy to take this to completion.

This has been narrated in the rabbit and tortoise story for over a century.

A tortoise with sustained energy to keep moving wins the race.

A talented person at a job not coupled with energy is a person who knows stuff but doesn't take things to completion. Here's a question for you. Does it really matter if that person was talented?

Energy is the least spoken word in the IT industry. However, the hidden secret behind every successful person is sustained energy to thrust beyond the series of excitement drops that are natural.

Football helps us learn this very well. It takes immense amounts of energy to score a goal. Before that one goal was scored, there have been times that the team took the ball near the goal a possible hundred times. At work, sometimes, we play a team sport and sometimes, we play an individual sport. One thing common is energy.

Energy has been one of the differentiators for Moolya. Our customers have asked us; how did you hire these good people? We hire people for energy. Skills can be learned, but energy can't.

People may end up thinking that introverts do not have energy and only extroverts have energy. Initial days of Moolya, Pradeep Soundararajan, Founder CEO of Moolya committed this sin. Thankfully, he stands corrected.

Irrespective of personality type, the ability to take things to completion is what determines who really has energy.

Discipline, why?

Discipline is a trait to consistently honour the commitment you made to yourself and others without needing a push from another person.

Everyone is disciplined by force. In the pretext of trying to teach discipline, many schools forced a routine on kids and called it discipline.

As adults, we make a lot of commitments to ourselves about reducing weight, eating less sugar, avoiding alcohol beyond a certain quantity, quitting smoking, to reduce screen time and we take our own commitment to ourselves for our benefit for granted. In this matter, we essentially treat others as we treat ourselves.

This is one of the reasons why many organizations felt a need to have a people manager whose job is to keep pushing people who aren't disciplined to be disciplined. This role is like the role of a circus master who has to get lions to behave in a certain way. The lion wants to eat that person every time they see him but can't.

Thankfully, the industry realized this role doesn't work and has largely removed it but that puts the onus on everyone to be self-disciplined. Money is one motivation why people who don't want to be disciplined, act disciplined and get things moving. Deadlines are another way to motivate people who don't want to do something by a certain time to finish the work. Appraisals are a reason why some people move when they don't want to move. Loans are another reason that has enabled people who lack discipline to act disciplined.

If deadlines, loans and money problems are removed, we would really know how poorly disciplined most of us are. Interestingly, those who don't have money problems and deadlines are those who are disciplined.

Discipline is also another reason why many people, despite aspirations to be rich, retire their thoughts because they realize that it demands discipline out of them. Discipline (or the lack of it) is also the same reason why people are happier to spend money on medical help than for improving their health.

Disciplined people prevent bad things from happening to themselves and others around them.

Disciplined product and engineering practices prevent thousands of bugs.

Disciplined execution saves plenty of money for organizations.

Presentability, why?

Presentability is not a fancy dress competition.

Presentability is two things in Moolya:

1. Not distracting people

2. Being able to influence people

Again, the word, presentability, makes people think it is about the dress. Yes, it can be but there are many other things that matter to presentability. The way we present our reports. The way we present our emails to others. The way we present in a meeting. The way we present our work and that of our colleagues.

A poorly formatted email often looks like a less credible one to pay attention to. A poorly drafted report removes the focus away from helping people make decisions based on the report. Great employees are those who can influence. This is true in every organization.

Moolya is Moolya because it has enough people who can influence and one of them is presentability. When Dhanasekar Subramaniam does mindmaps – it is clean, and distraction and clutter free. It brings focus to where it needs to go. He has coached many testers globally on mind mapping at international conferences and one thing he focuses on is the presentability of the mind maps.

Presentability goes a long way in influencing

99% of the JDs don't mention the word "influence." However, that is what everyone in the org is expected to do as an outcome of their work. Influence and impact are two things testers should chase about the value they contribute. Otherwise, they age and don't age well.

All people in all functions need presentability to themselves and their work. A bad presentation of an outbound email campaign to prospective customers can put the brand of Moolya down. An incorrect presentation of the numbers from the Finance team can cause an incoherent understanding of finance. A bad first-time presentation to a candidate might make Moolya less attractive for them to join.

Sometimes, people wonder that they put in a lot of hard work but aren't getting the desired results. It is simple, the blind spot is in the presentation of their hard work.

During a consulting assignment, Pradeep Soundararajan, presented 2 bugs as critical and he sure shot knew the stakeholders would accept it and fix it. He then said, "These 2 critical bugs came by because these 8 major issues were not fixed and it can happen again if we don't fix these 8 major issues." The stakeholders prioritized all issues reported by Pradeep. Even the minor ones.

Typically, people would end up presenting all the bugs they found in the report. However, they are making it hard for people to respond because it is too much to think about. Making it simple, presentable, clean and focusing on what matters first is what Pradeep did in the above example.

Most good people do a lot of hard work and succumb to presentability because that is easy to compromise when presenting a ton load of hard work. Also, presentations are done at the end of hard work so most people will be fatigued causing them to compromise their presentability.

Appreciation, why?

Big things get appreciated. Small things don't.

Many good things people do actually go unnoticed.

Why does this happen?

Everyone is busy moving things that need to be moved.

Everyone is in a fast-moving car and no one has the time to slow down and appreciate the beauty of the flower that just bloomed.

Our job involves giving and taking feedback.

We often forget that appreciating things that have moved with someone's help is part of feedback too. We only do that when:

    a. They have resigned and are moving out

    b. When people die suddenly

    c. When the pressure is off and we are drunk

    d. Because they appreciated us

    e. They saved our life

    f. They gave us a lot of money

As funny as it sounds, we aren't trained to appreciate and express our gratitude unless something big happens to us.

Appreciation is not a treasure to unlock it at events. Appreciation is like a compliment people want to give. People feel the need but don't do it.

For testers, to influence developers and decision-makers, appreciating people for the right thing matters. This helps build a bond as much as achieving results together does.

We all are focusing towards building quality and values. Appreciating people for small things at the right time helps them understand that even if there is no reward for doing some things, it matters to people around them. It is a deep positive reinforcement to help them do better and make everyone's life easier to achieve quality and values.

Sounds great on paper but how do we notice those small things?

Being conscious helps be observant all day. This doesn't come easily. This comes to those who develop second-order thinking. This also applies to those who meditate, practice mindfulness and so on. Most people are so glued to their phones that they haven't had a moment to feel or observe themselves.

There is another option in Moolya.

Moolyans, as per a specific policy, can apply to an observational holiday with the intent to observe, appreciate and help others succeed.

What can they do with observational holidays?

Plan a one-day leave in advance.

Just be logged in to work and observe what people are doing and just ask why they are doing what they are doing. Observe things that deserve appreciation and things that should be changed. Write appreciation emails but send them the next morning or get them scheduled for the next day.

Drop a note to the lead and manager on what was observed and what can be changed for the ease at which the product and quality can be built. Accountability is the key.

Once observation and consciousness kick in, every day becomes an observation day while working.

Clarity, why?

Clarity looks like a wish list but is not. Clarity is the ability to think without thinking of hypothetical situations that might impede moving from point A to B.

Here's how mind voice works for many people in cultures that blame each other, "I haven't finished this task and if I tell this in the stand-up meeting tomorrow morning, I will be questioned and looked upon as someone who didn't do work. Also, the last time when this happened to my colleague, she was hurt by a statement made by someone in the team. I fear this might happen to me and hence, what kind of answers should I prepare to counter the questions that might come my way?"

Such people aren't focusing on the core problem to be solved. Even in that case, clarity is,

"I don't have control over what people say about this information but hey, I said yes to requests that came in between and hence I couldn't finish. I am going to say that."

Clarity is thinking constraint-free. 99% of the things our minds imagine don't happen.

Clarity is available to seekers.

Those who enjoy their mind's voice and imagining hypothetical situations always move slowly.

Again, it doesn't matter what their talent is.

Many people who move things are oblivious to simple things like their thinking pattern is what makes them good. They always end up attributing everything to skills.

Less the ego, more the clarity.

Less the ego, more the clarity, better a team member.

The less the ego, the more the clarity, the better a team, the better a leader.

Problem-solving, why?

Isn't this obvious? No, it is not.

Most people solve a symptom of the problem and not the problem itself.

Here's an example:

When a bug is found in production – the common wisdom says – let us add a test to ensure this bug doesn't repeat in production. This is an example of surface-level problem-solving.

Root Cause Analysis might reveal the real problem is the cascading effect of a few bugs that were not fixed that caused this. So, if those bugs are fixed, the bug should be taken care of. Otherwise, a dead test keeps running for a long that has no use to it. The only exception where the cost of building the test, maintaining it, and running it far outweighs the cost of the bug in production. Even in that case, RCA and fixing cascading things matter. Maybe there are tests needed at the unit and integration level and not an automated end-to-end UI test.

Here is another example:

In the past, an early-stage funded startup approached Moolya for load and performance testing for a concurrency of 10k active sessions. 99% of the companies would have jumped in and said, "Let us do it for you" and slapped an invoice. Moolya did a deep dive study to find out the context they are in; they don't need it right now. However, they need something else. They needed support to improve their customer onboarding experience and we helped them fix that. Once they were getting a certain scale, we did help them with load and performance testing.

Doing just what the customer asked us to do would have not helped them solve their customer onboarding problem.

Is problem-solving a skill?

Yes and No.

Problem solving requires skills but problem solving per se is not a skill.

We as an industry try to put everything a person needs to do a great job as a skill.

The ability to identify what the problem really is a skill.

Book recommendation to Moolyans: "Are your lights on?" - Gerald M Weinberg (a.k.a Jerry Weinberg) available in Moolya library.

Jerry Weinberg has laid out simple approaches to finding out what the problem is, whose problem it is and how to help people and yourselves solve problems in that wonderful book.

Moolyans, irrespective of their role, are expected to develop second-order thinking, observation and objectivity to become good at identifying what the problem really is and address it.

Failures

We love to talk about failures. Our Moolyans are sharing the success of Moolya culture with their friends, family and over social media.

One of our customers asked us, "How can we build a culture like Moolya where people share their experiences on social media too?"

Moolyans also bring their family members and make them Moolyans. We have had sisters work together, brother sister work together, husband and wife work together (without any fights, of course) and even twins joining Moolya. Must be a good place. Yet, failures do happen and we continue to learn.

Equally, having a great culture does not mean it works all the time. In no company in the world, it works 100%.

Fun is our culture

Moolyans do have a lot of fun. Moolyans do party. Moolyans do have outings. Not that other companies don't. Moolyans do have a lot of fun at their workplace too without the need for our People teams to organize it. There is a lot of talk, laughter, dance and liveliness at our workplaces.

Sometimes, people have gotten carried away that having fun is what culture is. They think that is what defines Moolya culture.

Here is a non-obvious thing about fun – it means different things to different people. Some people have fun by listening to music and working. Some people have fun hacking code. That is what Moolya recognizes and is making the culture inclusive to all kinds of people to have fun in their own ways.

It is important to be mindful that having fun is necessary in everything we do and that is when life's experience is enhanced but if we make fun a blocker for progress, we aren't going to have two things in our life – progress and fun.

Fear is contagious as much as courage is

50% of the Moolyans are home grown. That means, we take freshers and train them to be a Moolyan. Most people take anywhere between 6 months to 2 years to imbibe the full Moolya value. We also hire laterals. We bring outliers, misfits, passionate people and people who are genuinely interested in being part of Moolya. We also hire Leads and Managers laterally as much as we home-grow them too.

Sometimes it happens that - people who join us, carry baggage from one of the previous stints where they had a culture of driving people through fear. No matter what we talk to them about the culture of Moolya, these people still have the baggage of fear.

Someone who joined us as a Lead was technically good but was carrying the baggage of

"What would people say if things went wrong?" Working with this Lead, the team started exhibiting fear. This got us in a spot where we weren't delivering the full Moolya value to our customer. These are things no company can find while interviewing. We didn't lose confidence in this person, instead, we helped this person understand our culture once again. We are okay with things going wrong but we are not okay with people not learning from it. No one should be okay with repeating failures. So, we helped this person feel safe to go ahead and be courageous and the team reciprocated too. Thankfully, this could be course-corrected when we found it early. If the team and lead lived in fear for over a year, it would be hard to get them out of it.

To prevent this from happening again, we implemented multiple systems that do dipstick tests as to how people are feeling and acting. Anything caught early can be fixed easily. Be it a bug or people's behaviour that is incongruent to the culture of Moolya.

Compromise of culture during pressure situations

Reminding you of our preamble, there shall be pressure. Under pressure - many good people will crack and appear as bad to people around them. Our culture definition and practices are aimed to help people operate calmly and objectively during pressure situations and hence, be useful in solving problems and making progress. Equally, making progress without getting frustrated has a direct impact on the health of people.

No matter how much we train people, sometimes, they like to throw their weight and ego around. This is human. Not about Moolyans. This is *Hooman* nature. Moolyans are oriented, trained, and reminded (almost in every alternate townhall) to not throw their weight around.

This is the level of intensity we as an organization put to help people focus instead of get emotional about things. Yet, once in a while, people crack up under pressure.

Once, a team failed in something. There was a person assigned to help the team not repeat the failure. The failure repeated. This person assigned to help them out got frustrated with the repetition of the failure and shot a strong email at this team. This hurt some people in the team and they wanted to quit instantly.

As a part of Moolya culture, we are intolerant of people repeating mistakes. No doubt or change in that but that does not warrant throwing weight around to solve a problem.

Here's how a solution to this problem, the Moolya culture way, looks like:

Have a simple list of RCA questionnaire:

- Did the team put in an effort to not repeat the mistake?

- Are they failing to ask for help?

- Are they understaffed?

- Are they saying Yes to something they should not?

- Do they know how to solve this problem?

- Did they know to spot a problem when it was happening?

- Are there too many things on their plate?

- Are we providing the support they need to not repeat this mistake?

The above questions are not philosophical questions. They are simple questions whose answers are Yes/No. Based on answers to these questions (and more such), either the matter has to be escalated or a decision needs to be made to rotate people or bring in new team members. If there is one person who has been negligent or lazy which causes the rest of the team to fail, then it is a simple decision to let go of this person after the first warning. Throwing weight and ego at people is easy but is also a way to become less influential in the long run.

Using culture as a protection against feedback

A rich culture suffers one known problem. When some people are being given feedback, they can easily put the blame on the culture not being inclusive to them and prevent feedback towards them.

This happened twice. When a leader called for a structured feedback meeting towards their reportee, in between the meeting the reportee said, "This feedback goes against the culture of Moolya and hence, this needs to stop right now."

This was then escalated, and on an investigation, found out that the reportee was trying to use Moolya Culture as a shield to prevent any feedback coming to them that challenges their image of themselves.

Sometimes, people assume that the feedback being given to them is to hint at a possible let go. Not true at all. Moolya is highly committed to helping people succeed. Not let them repeat their failure by bringing them the coaching they need and other support systems. In cases where people resist learning or lack the commitment to learn is when the decision to let go makes sense. Otherwise, feedback is part and parcel of anyone's life and career.

In any sport you take, a champion or a champion team also fails. If they resist feedback, they will never get back to being a champion again. For example, the below graph is the batting performance in Tests of Sachin Tendulkar who achieved the status of God in Cricket.

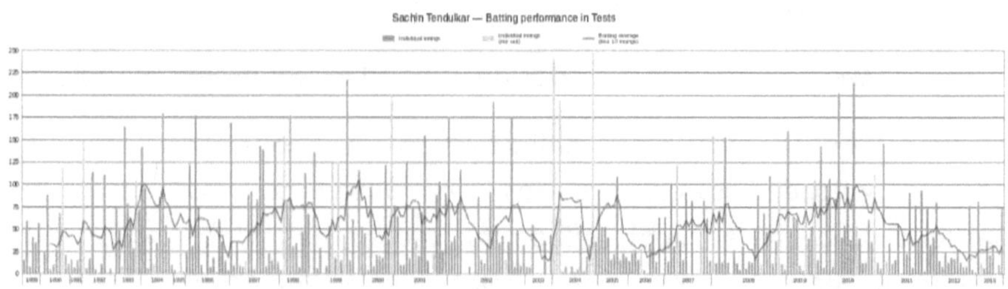

Source: https://commons.wikimedia.org/wiki/File:Sachin_Tendulkar_graph.svg

It is absolutely clear from the graph that the batting average keeps dropping in the career but the ability to lift it up again and again is what makes Sachin Tendulkar who he is. Had Sachin not been open to feedback both during times when he was doing great and when he was not doing great - the world would have not given him the God status in Cricket.

Customer's culture as a blocker

Moolya is able to be one of the most culturally rich companies in the world not just because of Moolyans but also because of the customers. We carefully choose our customers as much as they carefully choose us. Our customer's culture matters a lot to us. Moolya has positively influenced the culture of the customers many times and our customers have loved us for it.

However, Moolya has been in the business long enough to see things. There were very few instances over a decade where our customer's culture forced people to behave in a certain way, blame each other, defend themselves for every action or politicize the environment around them.

We take culture seriously. There are many ways to make money in life but most of us have chosen ethical, legal and professional ways to make it. That way, there are many ways to behave and work with other people. The Moolya Culture is a progressive way of working with fellow human beings and making great progress towards our customer's customers.

In one case, we escalated to our customer in a helpful way about their culture at a C level. They instantly acknowledged it and started taking action. They got back to us saying that beyond the valuable testing service we provided, they loved the fact that Moolya had a positive influence on the whole company.

In another case, when we brought the culture issues to the notice of a leadership team of our customer, they said; this is the culture we want to build and we are not going to change it because it is working for us.

We ended up being a technical fit but a cultural misfit. So, we decided to end the engagement to help our people not be too influenced by that culture. We respect their decision to remain who they are because everyone has a choice and the only question is are we a fit in such cases?

Moolya culture is not for everyone

Here is an email from someone who got it.

A note of Repentance from an Ex-Moolyan `External` Inbox

Removed <removed@gmail.com>   Oct 18, 2022, 6:11 PM
to me

Hi Pradeep,

Greetings for the day!

This is Removed, An Unlucky and Unfortunate Ex-Moolyan.

Back in 2021, I had decided to Part ways with Moolya after spending 2+ years of Valuable and Most memorable time at Moolya.
At that moment, compensation was the only criteria for me to move away from Moolya as my situation was demanding a big rise in my salary. And I had also thought of exploring other places of work and their culture apart from Moolya.

But after almost 2 years of journey away from Moolya, even though I have learnt and gained knowledge on many things, its been quite hard for me to find and be in a company which has the culture as of Moolya and I've been badly missing working at Moolya since two years. To be very honest, Moolya is one among very few companies which stands on top in respecting and taking care of an **Employee's Personal life**, and **family wellness**, among the companies I have worked with.

Work days used to be very peaceful during the days I worked with Moolya and there was no place for Unnecessary stress which used to impact the work efficiency.
This is the best thing about working in any company and I'm not enjoying the work currently upto the extent which I used to enjoy when I was at Moolya.

Also, after working in other companies and being messed up in adapting myself to other ways of testing, I feel the Moolya way of testing was actually more helpful in the betterment of my thinking ability as a tester and I actually miss myself being a better tester than what I'm now in terms of Creative thinking despite learning some new technologies in the other good product companies where I have worked.

Considering all the above factors, I thought of trying to apply, if there is any opportunity to **rejoin** and continue to have a Long time relationship with the best place I have ever worked and hence thought of Penning this short note to you.

Please let me know if there is any opportunity at Moolya for me to **Rejoin** and press a **Re-start** button to my professional life. I will be prepared to undergo the further steps.

Attaching my resume to this email too.

(If there is any wrong usage of words/sentences in this note, please pardon. I assure you that the intention is very pure.)

Yours Sincerely,
Removed
Ex Moolyan and Wanna be Moolyan again.

The email was edited with Inspect Element and actual name, photo on profile and certain details removed to protect the identity of this person. This person was not removed from Moolya :)

This, indeed, is the best email any organization can receive from their ex-employee. This email is evidence that this person is still living in gratitude. That is beneficial to this person's health.

There is no HR in Moolya but there is a HR Ops Team. How?

Typically HR means Human Resources. The industry is plagued with people who think of humans as resources. This is an industry problem and not necessarily a people-specific problem. When people start their careers, if they are surrounded by people who keep referring to humans as resources, it is likely that they will pick this language and carry it throughout their career. They don't change.

Moolya does not subscribe to the thought of humans to be referred to as resources. If true, why do we then have an HR team? The HR in HR Ops stands for Human Relations.

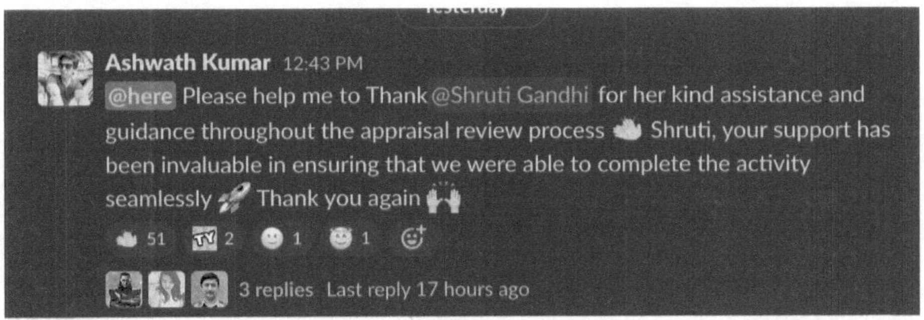

Screenshot from our Slack #kudos channel

This is what Human Relations look like in Moolya. The HR ops team took care of helping people succeed in the appraisal review process and helped leaders build deeper relationships with their reportees.

Typically, the appraisal process is a daunting task on all sides. The way our Human Relations team (HR of Moolya) functions is by enabling people to deal with things in the most humane way possible. The Human Relations team enables Moolyans to have a holistic growth appraisal process. Not just on work but holistic progress of life and work. This is in line with the culture of Moolya.

Equally bringing to your notice. The #kudos channel has been a great way that Moolyans appreciate each other and is in line with the "Appreciation" part of our Moolya culture. There is no one's approval required to appreciate anyone in the #kudos channel. Small things get appreciated by colleagues, peers and leaders on this channel in front of everyone in Moolya. Expressing gratitude makes a person healthy and live a good long life. The culture of Moolya is designed for a good long holistic life.

Policy making and adherence in Moolya

The Human Relations Team is in charge of creating, maintaining and helping the company follow helpful policies drafted. The way policies are made is also holistic in nature. It is a balance of business and people. Typically, the leadership team of any organization is involved in policy making and the employees of the organization have to just follow.

Moolya being *moolya (meaning value)*, about 5 years ago, opened up all policies for comments and feedback to everyone in Moolya and many policies went through changes and updates based on feedback from Moolyans. Similarly, customer, culture, leadership team and Moolyans have helped shape the policies.

This holistic approach by the Human Relations team to policy making and enabling adherence at the ground level is what helps Moolya stand out.

That said, in a constantly evolving world, the new policies that are made and the old ones being updated to suit the modern-day world are important for any organization. Moolya Human Relations Operations team has been a team that has been open and incorporates modern-day needs into Moolya's policies.

Collaboration in policy-making and adherence to the policies by Moolyans is the reason why Moolya has been able to scale and function smoothly.

Build your own Moolya within Moolya

The shareholders, board and CXOs of Moolya consist of entrepreneurs. They totally support entrepreneurship. Moolyans, after gaining a significant depth of experience and wanting to create value as an entrepreneur, can do so with the support system of Moolya.

We are not glorifying entrepreneurship by saying that. We are just saying that there are 2 kinds of people. Those who create value and those who build value. They need each other. Just creators without builders won't succeed. No people or less or more than the other. However, creation challenges a different set of muscles than the muscles 99% of the world is trained on. Most people are trained to be builders once the value is figured out.

Since it is a different muscle that will be challenged, support systems are needed to succeed during the initial stages to do heavy lifting. Otherwise, it can lead to muscle tears, injuries and accidents. Moolya has been able to grow because of the wisdom of the board and shareholders who have been in business long enough and have seen cycles of up and down and world economic changes long enough.

The learning that the CXOs have had from fellow entrepreneurs and the board of directors is funnelled in to help Moolyans succeed as entrepreneurs within the ecosystem of Moolya but in their own company and freedom.

Startups by Moolyans

Perfachhi by Abilash Hari

Perfachhi is the easiest way to monitor app performance while testing. Abi has been part of Moolya for over 10 years now. During his 10-year stint, he has played several roles beginning as a Tester and then as a Trainee Product Manager, Product Manager and then as an entrepreneur of Perfachhi (funded and supported by Moolya)

Perfachhi is available today as an open-source tool at https://github.com/appachhi/perfacchi.android-sdk

This enabled him to function as Solutions and Pre-Sales Head of Moolya and he has done exceptional in this space.

Why is he exceptional?

He is exceptional because he wanted to be and worked to become one. Period. That said, while not taking credit away from him, Moolya chartered him to build different muscles. He was willing to take the help of Moolya. There are people who resist role changes and they even quit. They think their career would go for a toss. Abi didn't. He played several different roles that came his way to use that as an opportunity to see an overall development in skills.

What is the difference between Abi and others who have been in only testing roles for long?

Since Abi built Perfachhi which involved working with Google Developers Community. He developed skills to connect deeper with Product Owners and Developers. When Abi speaks to our customers, they listen to him. He has been able to influence different models that have helped our customers increase their revenue and grow faster by applying approaches to testing and preventing bugs. Our customers take advice from Abi seriously.

MoolyaEd by Amit Vyas

MoolyaEd is a great way for freshers to become industry-ready and for experienced folks to upskill themselves in niche areas. Amit joined Moolya as a Trainee Tester and presented at MITC (Moolya Internal Testing Conference). He had the skill to influence people and had the energy to create something. Apparently, he had built a startup while studying for his Bachelors and while he claims it failed, he didn't fail to learn from it. Amit, like Abi did, was willing to try different roles. He played a role in Sales for Moolya for a year. Timing was wrong but Amit didn't give up. He went on to play the role of a Test Lead for a project and built super credibility for Moolya. This diversity laid a foundation for him to see an opportunity for his own growth by helping Moolya's customers to scale faster. He built Moolya's fulfilment engine.

What's the difference between fulfilment and recruitment?

Amit and his wonderful team do recruitment and go beyond that to fulfil the open positions. What's the difference? Recruitment ends when a person is onboard but fulfilment ends only when the people hired have started to deliver. This also means coaching and mentoring the person to deliver value is a key part.

As a discovery into fulfilment, Amit realized the need to train people to make them more fulfilable. That's also how MoolyaEd was born. MoolyaEd is all set to train the future thousands of people with aspirations to get into testing and upskill those serious testers. MoolyaEd might venture into other areas in future but Amit is doing an excellent value creator role already with it. He is building partnerships and expanding his network. Amit can easily become one of the most influential people in transforming people's careers in Testing.

The impact MoolyaEd has on society is immense. Amit's podcasts are widely appreciated by expert testers in the industry and he is beginning to build a great community of people in tech, test and product through MoolyaEd.

https://www.moolyaed.com

CaaS by Chandini Mokthar

CaaS is Culture As A Service. If you have read the chapter on Culture prior to reading this, you would know how incredibly hard it is to define, set and practice culture for an organization. CaaS is a great support system for Founders and HRs to build a culture that helps fulfil the business vision and people vision for startups to medium-scale organisations.

Chandini joined Moolya as a Recruiter. Chandini cared enough about Moolya that over time, she was bringing in changes to the way things were happening and most importantly doing it in a calm, peaceful way. This was aligned with the founders' vision of what the culture of Moolya should be heading towards.

Equally, people loved interacting with Chandini. She was a real problem solver. She has solved personal, professional and interpersonal problems that people have brought up to her. This led to influencing people to behave, think and act in a certain way that is helpful to them.

http://moolyacaas.com

What led Chandini to build CaaS?

At one point, Chandini was responsible for everything. When Moolya started to grow, she spotted inefficiencies in too many things she was doing and decided to build teams and let go of certain responsibilities to focus more and more on People.

Chandini, as all of us, had her apprehensions about letting things go but it is because of that many great things happened to Moolya. She built a wonderful team that is delivering great experience to Moolyans.

Despite all the failures we have spoken about in this book, people are having a great experience and they often share this internally or publicly. This has led many of our customers to be excited about our culture and ask us more about our culture.

Where did the need come from?

A CEO even asked, "Can Moolya help us set up our culture?" and this led Chandini to explore the market need in this space and most companies' HR Consultancies help in setting up the Operations side of things for People and not Culture.

Chandini and her team who have seen large-scale People and Culture challenges and solved problems and prevented many are well poised to help customers of CaaS prevent many mistakes in setting up and implementing a good culture in their org.

The founders of Moolya wish they had such a service they could have used right from inception.

They are glad now this service shall help plenty of companies to go ahead of Moolya.

Moolya Dev by Avinash Nishant

Avinash Nishant became a co-founder and partner to Moolya several years after Moolya was founded. Avinash's background is programming. He loves to automate stuff. Not the test automation part but anything that can be automated. His first startup, Kiranawala, was an e-commerce delivery for groceries in 2010. He had a brilliant execution but couldn't raise VC money because he was way ahead of the time. The Venture Capitalists told him this model won't work. They said people in India won't buy groceries online and then funded other companies later.

He then pivoted to build Shopnix which caters to a niche segment of the market to build e-commerce. Pradeep Soundararajan pitched to him the idea of building A.I. driven Automation which attracted Avinash to join hands with Pradeep and build AppAchhi. 3 years into the journey - Pradeep and Avinash built a great partnership and Avinash coming on board of Moolya was imminent.

What is Moolya Dev and how does this align with Moolya's vision?

By the time Avinash came on board, Moolya knew that the vision of Preventing Bugs was only possible when we worked closely with Product Owners, CTOs, Architects and Developers. Moolya also learnt the challenge of building unit tests and integration tests that customers have while developing.

Moolya Dev has two goals. Build test-savvy product developers and build a service to clear tech debt. These are two top reasons bugs prevent the growth of a company.

Cleaning code is the hardest job in the world. That is why people choose to live with bugs. When poorly unit-tested and poorly undocumented code becomes legacy, it becomes a pain to maintain it.

What is the secret ingredient to Moolya Dev?

People. The success of anything Moolya is people. Avinash brought in a wonderful set of Developers with him. They were handpicked and trained by Avinash on principles of engineering that have helped them build scale-able code with very little tech debt and fewer bugs.

This is what Avinash wanted to offer as a service to customers of Moolya and he tested waters with a few customers and they instantly liked this problem statement to be solved. We now have Moolya Dev as a fast-growing business unit within Moolya.

Without Avinash and his team and their combined entrepreneurial spirit to create value for Moolya Customers, Moolya Dev would have not been possible. Avinash credits his team of developers, Sudhir Reddy and Mohammed Irfan, who are leading this effort.

Bugasura by Avinash Nishant, Rapti Gupta, Sourabh Kanchibail

Bugasura is a modern-day bug tracker for SaaS teams. Most bug trackers that startups and enterprises use are decades old and built for enterprises to micro-manage people. They are complex, slow and a chore to operate. To the extent that people list it as a skill.

Sourabh has been with Moolya for over 7 years helping build several tools and running experimental product-building activities while also getting involved in building AppAchhi. Rapti Gupta joined the Bugasura team directly as a Founding Member when Avinash Nishant and Pradeep confessed to each other that they didn't know Product Marketing. Added to them, the designers and the dev team building Bugasura also have a long history with Moolya. Most of them have spent at least 4-6 years with Moolya.

Bugasura became the #1 Product of the Day in Product Hunt and even prior to that, Bugasura enjoys an international customer base. People report bugs in Spanish, Arabic, Bahasa Indonesia, Thai, German, Italian, Hindi and English. Global teams that collaborate remotely use Bugasura. That's how spread out the customer and user base is.

What's modern and unique about Bugasura?

Everything is unique about Bugasura. The way we think of a bug tracker, the way we build, the experience, the use cases we think of and the value our customers and users are deriving out of it.

Bugasura engineering and design principles

- Adding features is easy so let us do it when absolutely necessary

- After every 3 new "add feature" sprints there is a "remove and clean" sprint

- People should not think of doing something

- The core goal of Bugasura is to help people close bugs faster

- We extensively use our own product to build our product

- Simplicity is a USP

- Everything we build must have simplicity as the USP

- Remove stuff that is not simple

- Deepen the love of existing users than build new features to get new customers

- Design has to translate into experience

- Speed and performance are equally important to functionality

- A feature is only complete when it is simple, usable and has a fast response rate

- Prevent bugs

- Remove features that are not used

- Keep cleaning the code

- Talk to customers – do plenty of demos

Given that this is what we follow and see a robust quality in the product, it helps us advise Moolya's customers right. It helps us show credibility that we speak from practice and not what we have heard work for others or a best practice shared at a conference. We are also context-aware of when this works and when this does not, and hence, we have solutions to get the readiness for our customers to help them succeed.

Future startups and plans

Entrepreneurship is gaining good momentum globally and yet, there is a high mortality for early-stage startups. Equally, Moolya being committed to holistic growth thinks the immense stress founders go through isn't worth the returns. Moolya is an incubator for startups that Moolyans and non-Moolyans want to build in the space of engineering and quality.

We also hope to set up a fund for incubating startups that focus on building engineering and quality-related products and services. We also look forward to providing them with office space and support to get them off the ground faster. We believe that every organization should turn into an incubator and help promote innovation. Again, as a reminder, creators and builders are of equal value and are complementary to each other.

CHAPTER 9

Career Transformation Programs

Career Transformation

We strongly believe that people are in search of a transformation. They are not in search of another job. Many times, money blinds them to think if someone is offering more money it must be transformational to their life. Once they spike their expenses up, the extra money fades away and again they are back to job hunting. Yet, this cycle never appears to end.

One cannot transform themselves by job hopping. They can, at best, change the problem statement and the money but after they have hit saturation point, the focus moves away from everything else to what they have truly become.

Moolya is keen to help people transform their lives. If you have come here after reading the chapter of Startups by Moolyans, you would agree that one type of transformation is enabled by Moolya. Here are other ways that Moolya enables career transformation for people.

Not everyone wants to be an entrepreneur. We get it. People should absolutely not do something just because it is sexy to do it or everyone is doing it. Everyone has a gift deep inside. We believe when people discover their gift, they should bring the gift out and put it to the use of this world.

For instance, the gift Avinash Nishant, CTO and COO of Moolya has, is to be able to break down any complex problem into simple executable pieces and track it to closure. This has helped him become a great programmer and build scalable high-quality software.

One could be doing great but be a misfit

Dhanasekar has a gift to coach and mentor testers to succeed. He has helped hundreds of testers in Moolya to do better. Dhanasekar wasn't in a coaching role. He was in a Delivery role. He was not liking it one bit. He liked the testing part but didn't like the operations, metrics, numbers, or P&L responsibility. When he said Yes to that role, he didn't know what was coming but he tried the role and figured out the immense value he could bring in as a coach for testers in Moolya.

Today, he is in a full-time role that involves coaching and consulting testers and leaders in Moolya who need help to succeed. A transformation for him was about moving away from delivery to a coaching and consulting role. Moolya is open to such changes as long as there is ROI on that role.

Anything a tester does should tie back to business value

Whatever role anyone is playing in an organization, there should be a valuable contribution to the business. If the value drops below the salary that is demanded, then it becomes unsustainable to retain them. This is the simple rule of business.

We think the business only understands:

- Product value - Are you helping the customer succeed in using the product?

- Tech value - Are you helping in building clean code or helping ship faster?

- Business value - Are you contributing to the top line or bottom line?

And they don't understand:

- Test value

Maybe the product and tech teams understand test value but the business does not. At least 95% of them don't. They have other things to take care of. Due to this reason, the business doesn't put a high ROI on testing and cost, growth, and salary decisions are made by the business. When they have to cut costs, it becomes convenient to cut a cost that they don't see a direct ROI on.

However, that does not mean business makes unilateral decisions. So, they always consult the Tech and Product teams before making a decision on testing. How strongly do Product and Tech teams vouch for testing depends on the value the test team is bringing to either of them.

So, testers have to be in 3 buckets:

- Strong customer revenue and bottom-line inclination

- Strong product value inclination

- Strong tech value inclination

If one is long enough in neither of these buckets, they end up waiting for when the time bomb stops ticking on their career growth. For instance, someone who says, "I am very good at coming up with test cases." Where do they really fit in? That may be a valuable asset to test value but the business thinks if there are great test cases and on the other side the customers are dropping out due to bugs, they don't care if there were great test cases in the org or not.

Business people only understand customers, revenue and profitability. That's it. We may want them to understand testing but that is like our pancreas asking us to understand how it works. Most of us don't. We take it for granted and move on. Of course, the pancreas is important but to live our lives we can without understanding how the pancreas works. It is also true that we may live a healthier life if we understand how the pancreas works but there are many who lived a good life on this Earth without knowing they had a pancreas. So, the business would ask, "What's the big deal if I don't know about testing if they can't translate their value to business value?"

People who think they are bringing tech value because they are writing automated tests are assuming that the tests are yielding business value. They may not be. Automated tests are those that need to be retired and new ones need to be introduced often. So, there is no permanent value to automated tests that we create. How do we then justify business value through the tech value of automated tests?

We know thousands of testers in the industry who don't interact with customers and users nor have looked into product usage analytics. They are doing a job. They think their job is to come up with tests, run them, automate them and be answerable to a release and firefight an issue in production. This is disastrous to their career in testing. They may be getting a hike year on year and even promoted. They are not adding any product tech or business value by doing so. They live life in regression created out of tech debt.

Having understood what Business, Product, Tech value and Test value is, we decided to help Moolya testers transform their career into deepening the value they can contribute to.

Why are many testers failing to discover their gift?

Most of us are gifted with something. Anyone who has worked for over 5-7 years has discovered something that they are naturally good at. It could be simple-looking things such as writing emails, facilitating a meeting, influencing someone to add a testability hook into the product, or writing a tool to automate test-related activities but not testing, documenting or formatting a test report.

Instead of building on top of it - the natural tendency of many people is to go build something that is helping everyone else get the next job. For instance, many learn automation in the fear that they might be left behind and not for the love of learning how to improve the feedback cycle to devs.

Committed to providing value, Moolya decided to help people build on what they are good at and came up with ways to help our testers succeed.

Business and Product Value Focus: BA in Testing

In partnership with the Institute of Product Leadership - Moolya L&D launched a program to help product-savvy folks within Moolya to learn Product Management and Data Analytics. IPL (Institute of Product Leadership) played a phenomenal role in enabling our product-savvy testers to learn to play the role of a PM. They brought in industry experts, their own alumni who are working as a PM and PO to coach our testers.

A program for 6 months that covers:

- Product Management Fundamentals

- UX/UI Design

- Data Analytics Foundation

- Data visualization

- Product Management for Digital Products

- Hands on practical projects

This enabled our testers to graduate from, "Hey, I think I am adding product value" to "Here is the product value I am bringing to the table" and influence Product Owners and Product Managers from our customers.

These testers now can do the following:

- Do product market fit assessments

- Do persona mapping

- Define MVPs

- Write epics and stories

- Wireframes

- Conduct user interviews

- Mind map

- Plot user journeys

- Demo to customers and users

- Define analytics for understanding user behaviour

This is super useful to speak the Product Owner's language. POs and PMs are 10 times more likely to be influenced by testers who can speak their language and help them out as to why certain issues are real blockers by showing how users will be blocked by it and the revenue delay or loss due to it.

This is revolutionary.

Moolya graduates these testers internally after successful course completion to Business Analysts in Testing and provides them opportunities in projects where the POs and PMs are aligned to bring such value on board. They are now a great blend of Product and Test value. The people who graduated from this course are contributing a phenomenally different value than what other testers are bringing to the table. Simple reason – depth.

Case study-

A certain US-based B2B company had a customer onboarding challenge. Their onboarding process took 8 to 10 weeks. When our BA in Testing Moolyans investigated the issue, they found out things that could be speeded up and worked with their product teams to bring down the onboarding process to 4-6 weeks. This means faster revenue realization.

One could ask, is this in the realm of testing? Our customer recognises this value is possible because people came from a testing background to do this. They internally have their own test team but to be able to see the customer onboarding challenge - the mindset required a combination of product team (that was understaffed there) and strong customer interaction and empathy mindset.

This customer is delighted. They give us a 5-star rating. We give them a 7-star rating for being open to help. In this tech world, people find it hard to seek help. The most successful people are those who take help to move forward and take everyone forward with them. This customer is adding customers consistently and growing rapidly. The CEO appreciated the value we are bringing to the table. The VP of Engineering and Product Owners love us.

Tech value: Moolya Developer in Test

Avinash Nishant had built developer training and onboarding into the product companies he built. There were two parallel things that happened when we came on board. Pradeep Soundararajan was exploring building unit testing as a service and tech debt clearance as a service, aligning with the vision of preventing bugs for Moolya customers. A counterintuitive service offering, actually. 2 of 3 CTOs he spoke to said while they want their developers to write unit tests – they don't write unit tests but would also resist the idea of another developer writing a unit test for their code.

This idea evolved to help developers clean the tech debt they were accumulating and it needed developers with a lot more discipline to be able to do the tech debt cleaning job.

Sounds like SDET? Although the original idea of SDETs was not for automation but today, the industry has made SDETs synonymous with automation. MDIT is committed to creating true SDETs and Product code-grade developers.

'The tech world may not publicly say it but here is a locker room talk - Automation Engineers and most SDETs are considered low-key programmers and not product developer grade developers. There are some exceptional SDETs whose code quality is on par or better than that of product developers but they are outliers. They don't make up the majority of the industry.

With Moolya Dev as well happening, Avinash and the L&D team of Moolya decided to lay a stronger foundation for those who are inclined to contribute to tech value and take them through the program designed to create product-grade developers with elements of test automation added to it. This became Moolya Developer in Test Program where programmers are created whose code quality, code commenting, and code review process is on par with good product developers.

The selection criteria are tough. People have to go through a programming mindset test. Some people who thought they had become good at automation couldn't clear and some who didn't realize the gift within themselves did.

These developers are trained to:

- Stick with the systematic process of thinking

- Think slowly

- Not yield to pressure

- Not take shortcuts that add tech debt

- Not skip steps to hit the deadline

- Not meeting a deadline at the cost of quality

- Value discipline of doing things

Quality can't always be met by meeting a deadline. Especially when we are in the service of cleaning up after someone hasn't had the luxury to pay attention to quality.

Career transformation for people in growth teams

Talking about holistic growth means thinking holistically too. The growth teams of Moolya are a combination of Fulfilment, Sales, Solutions and Operations. The philosophy of the core leadership team and the entrepreneurial mindset of growth teams is the core enabler of the growth of Moolya.

Moolya Core Leadership Team is of the belief that the people reporting to them should replace them in 3 years' time so that they can graduate to newer problem statements or build a Moolya complementary startup.

When people at the top (from a decision-making standpoint) want to vacate their seat for their reportee, that's usually a good spot for everyone to be. This means the core leadership team is constantly helping their reportees to become self-reliant and make decisions. This also means the core leadership team is constantly being challenged and new ideas flow in.

Here's a wonderful example. Gautam KR reports to Vaisakh VL (Sales Head). The way Vaisakh has supported Gautam and the way Gautam has taken ownership of things, 90% of the show that Vaisakh was running is not run by Gautam. This is in one year of Gautam joining us.

Similarly, with fulfilment. Amit Vyas (Head of Fulfilment) has brought in a wonderful team on board. They help each other succeed. Sushmitha who reports to Amit has taken more ownership that helped Amit be able to run Fulfilment and also in parallel be the Founder CEO of MoolyaEd.

These are brilliant stories. The leaders coach and mentor their reportees to grow and outgrow them. This is the DNA of Moolya. When people are exposed to such a leadership team, they just emulate what they have seen in practice.

Pradeep Soundararajan, Founder CEO, currently runs a mentoring program for the reportees of the Core Leadership team and focuses on holistic growth of themselves and learning to solve complex problems with maximum ease. Why ease? We all can break our heads and solve problems but as we continue to repeat it and we age, the stress builds up.

Rucha Jhadav came in as a management consultant 2 years ago and played the role of a generalist working with Pradeep Soundararajan. She kept wondering where her career was headed because her friends would say they were working on a specific project. She had her doubts but time answered questions for her. She is now Head of Storytelling for Moolya and her team is doing a fab job. She is doing a great job of influencing people and moving things.

The goal is to create a better replacement of the core leadership team and set a culture of core leadership early on 2 years before they all replace the core leadership team in the roles that are currently being played.

Added to all the above, there are several leadership courses and programs from various universities that are on offer for the growth teams from time to time. Life in growth teams is constant learning and holistic growth. Only for those who are hungry and not very foolish. :)

Chapter 10
Fulfilment

Fulfilment

We do fulfilment in Moolya.

What is the difference between Recruitment and Fulfilment?

Simple. Recruitment ends when the candidate joins the job after an offer. Fulfilment only ends when the candidate succeeds in the job. This goes a 100 kilometres beyond recruitment. That is why we have fulfilment teams and recruiters are a part of the whole process of fulfilment. This is good for the recruiters as well because they know their efforts are paying off larger dividends. This is good for candidates as well because they know there is a seriousness to them succeeding in the job that is put in rather than just bringing them on board.

Amit Vyas is the Founder of this concept in Moolya and has built a fantastic team to make this happen.

Fulfillment has 3 parts:

- Attracting talent

- Interview experience

- Placement

Attracting talent

We believe that 90% of the work is done by getting the right people to show interest in becoming a Moolyan. Our storytelling team backed by People and Fulfilment teams share stories on our social media that have brought thousands of talented people to apply to be a Moolyan. We call those who voluntarily want to become a Moolyan but not yet are as Woolyans (Wannabe- Moolyans)

Who we are is what attracts the kind of people who want to work with us. The ability to express who we are is what differentiates us from the rest of the employers for the candidate.

When we put a form out for people to apply for a specific role, when our recruiter puts a post out on Linkedin, when our Moolyans share about the jobs to their friends, in everything, there has to be a touch of who we are. The power of the subconscious is such that the voice deep inside the candidate says, "This is your place" and when candidates apply with a conviction like that, we often end up working together as fellow Moolyans.

Interview experience

We put depth and empathy into our interview process to onboard Noolyans (New Moolyans). For Moolya, everyone we interact with is our customer. The candidates we interview, our Moolyans, our partners, our suppliers and our customers are all customers. We are here to serve them an experience and exchange an experience that is rewarding.

Interviews are also a great way to build relationships. We have had immense appreciation coming from candidates who went through our interview experience irrespective of whether they received an offer or not. This is possible when they feel they had a conversation about their fitment rather than being judged for their skills. Also, interviewing is stressful for candidates and we totally understand it. That is why we want to help make it a very comfortable experience for them.

Moolya recruiters and the magic they create

Our Fulfillment Team has some fantastic people from the recruitment space. These people are full of life. That is why when they make the first call to the candidate to pitch Moolya, the candidates many times have felt a fresh breath of air.

Moolya recruiters go through an orientation process with the Moolya way of recruitment. There are guidelines on screening, shortlisting, communicating with candidates and helping them throughout the experience from the first call to the offer to joining.

Rather than looking at them as recruiters, the CXOs of Moolya look at them as people who sell the vision of Moolya to potential Moolyans.

Why do the CXOs of Moolya care about recruitment? That is because their job is recruitment too. They are in constant recruitment of people who can help Moolya grow. Back in 2011, when Moolya was operating out of a garage the call went like this, "Hey, this is Pradeep Soundararajan. I am the Founder CEO of Moolya. Am I speaking to XXXX and do you have a few minutes to talk about a possible opportunity to come and be a part of a huge vision?" followed up by, "We want to tell this to you upfront. We operate out of a garage. So, you walk in - you won't see a corporate office. A garage. No meeting rooms. The interview would happen where everyone else is. Are you comfortable to work in such an environment?"

There were many who declined to be interviewed by us after hearing that. There were even candidates who would come, peep in and run away. Sales teams and Recruitment teams live in rejection. This builds a certain muscle in them that makes them comfortable hearing plenty of 'Nos' every day and yet have their confidence levels unaffected.

The founders, founding team and CXOs have done recruitment for many years and are still taking care of the end-to-end experience of senior leadership hiring.

That said, the recruiters in Moolya play a pivotal role in increasing the scale of an organization. They have been able to scale the value set by the core leadership team. They do this consistently and with joy. The most important piece being joy.

They have a set of guiding principles and pointers on how to:

- Shortlist

- Connect

- Build and manage the experience of the candidate

- Offer rollout

- Handover

Without the kind of recruiters we have, it would be impossible to see the vision and culture turning into reality. They also take feedback from the candidates about their end-to-end experience and bring in improvements to what values and principles we already have. A true mark of co-ownership.

The magic they create with the candidates can be put in one word – Partnership. The candidate feels they can rely upon this recruiter they are speaking with to help them find an answer to the question they have in their mind. If the answer is No. The candidates know that they would rather hear it from someone with empathy than those without it.

Interviewers and their key role

Many interviewers across the globe have no time to read the JD or the profile of the candidate they are interviewing. This is sad. They arrive at the interview table without having spent enough time preparing for the interview. In Moolya, we did not want candidates to go through this experience.

Equally for interviewers, their life experience is enhanced when they build relationships and discover new people in their lives. Every interaction is an exciting possibility in life. Interviewers have to see interviews as a way of "giving" to the world. Why? Interviews are life-changing for people. To the interviewer as well because it is an opportunity to meet future teammates who can come and influence the way they do things. How should we take a life-changing experience? With seriousness and excitement.

Interviewers in Moolya are trained on:

- How to prepare for the interview?

- How to help the candidate get to ease?

- How to enable candidates to ask questions?

- How to listen to candidates?

- How to assess fitment?

- How to discover if the candidate can take feedback or not?

- How to help the candidate?

- How to not be carried away in the process of asking questions?

All this combined with our culture, values and empathy, our interviewers have brought in some wonderful talent onboard. For candidates, interviewers are actual people they are going to work with. So, our offer acceptance ratio and joining ratio tell us volumes about how our interviewers are doing a great job of demonstrating Moolya values.

Interviewers are also reminded that:

- We are not judging candidates

- We are at best assessing fitment to the role available

- Don't look for perfect-match candidates

- Cultural fitment is absolutely essential

- Don't bring on board a tech genius who is egoistic with people

Our interviewers get an extra bonus for conducting good interviews. Rewarding people for the right thing helps aspirant interviewers within Moolya to mimic the behaviour of successful interviewers. The culture of interviewing is grown by the interviewers as aspiring interviewers shadow a seasoned interviewer to learn the nuances of how to be an interviewer – the Moolya Way.

Empathy

Right from 2011, we built a culture of giving a Thank You card to everyone who interviewed with us and the interviewer signing a best wishes on the card. This was loved by candidates. For those who travel to come and meet us, this was a simple gesture that brightened the day. Post-pandemic, this card is going online.

Equally, candidates without a job (after having built an experience) were even eligible to get their travel partially reimbursed. We have had some candidates who were jobless shed a tear of joy when we asked them – would you like to be reimbursed for coming over to meet us today?

Feedback and communication with candidates

As much as we seek feedback from candidates, we want to provide feedback to them to help them succeed. For instance, if someone claims they have a certain skill thinking that is what would get them a job versus them not realizing they have a superpower elsewhere, we want to help them realize what they should focus on.

Not everyone is wired in their brain to take feedback although they ask for it. It becomes very tricky to provide feedback. Some people fall in deeper love with us when we share it and some people start abusing us. Our philosophy is to not provide anything from our ego perspective or to make someone feel bad. However, emotions are very high for people desperate to get a job and we understand that. So, we listen to them and be calm. It doesn't matter who is right in such a situation. It matters who is calm and what the final result is.

Here's an actual email sent to applicants on March 24th for a Marketing Head position for Bugasura, our Founder CEO opened and closed.

excerpt begins

Greetings!

I want to personally thank you for applying to this position that we had an opening for. I read through every response in detail, at least twice. Why twice? I wanted to give it a second thought to see if I were to change my understanding. I did not judge anyone's form response.

That said, anyone who has spent their time applying deserves feedback and I thought let me make it generic so that it helps everyone here apply better next time to another company.

Here is a quantitative summary first

- There were in total 56 responses

- 30% of them were women and 70% were men

- 60% of them who applied have 6 years or lesser industry experience

- People had applied from at least 9 different cities

- 94% of them had worked with a startup before

- Among applicants the specialization people mentioned was

  - Running campaigns was 34%

  - Leading marketing teams was 34%

  - Content Distribution was 14%

  - The rest were minor percentages

- 58% of the applicants didn't have a mentor

- 75% of the applicants were mentoring someone else though

Here is a qualitative summary:

- 40% of the applicants hardly put in an effort to understand and answer the questions. Most of the responses were a single word or a single line for questions about failure. This was a key aspect of filtering. Your failures tell more about what you tried with your career than success actually does sometimes.

- More than 75% of people lacked a detailed explanation as to why people liked to work with them.

- 10% of the people put in as much effort as I put in to make the form. They demonstrated that they cared to put in an effort to apply. I spent an hour and a half writing the form. Maybe others too wanted to do it but were filling in their busy schedule.

Interview process and selection

- I shortlisted 4 people to speak to.

- I felt the 4 had demonstrated depth in their answers.

- I decided to speak to them one by one in serial rather than parallel.

- If one rejects the offer or doesn't work out then move to the next.

- It was a tough bet.

- I had short-listed someone who had spent 7 years at the same org growing from junior to a Director of Marketing. Not because she spent 7 years there but the energy she carried along from her application to the conversations we had on the phone.

- With her, the most important question was why bootstrapped company? The clarity of her suitability was phenomenal.

- I immediately followed up with other rounds and a face-to-face discussion.

- 2 weeks.

- If she said No or we said No, I was 2 weeks slower.

- Why didn't I talk to others? Careful of giving people hope. Everyone's disappointed if time is spent and no result happens.

- All worked between us and our new Head of Marketing and today, the offer was rolled out and she has accepted it officially too.

Why am I sharing this with you?

- To tell you that I missed the opportunity to talk to you.

- Also, if this email was of any help, I would feel good I wrote this to you.

- However, I want to keep in touch with you if you are on Linkedin, please send me a request with a note that you had applied to this role and I will add you.

- I have other opportunities coming up and I think I know who to talk to now.

- I wanted to express my gratitude and thanks to you for considering working with us.

- Please continue to support us and continue to wish for we never know when we might work together again.

- Also, wish the person who is joining us a good journey with us. This is a life-changing moment for us.

Gratitude,

Pradeep Soundararajan,

Chief Servant to Employees and Customers | Founder CEO

excerpt ends

For sending the above email, we received both: deep love messages and messages that were written out of emotion of not being shortlisted for an interview. Someone took it personally that individual-level feedback was not provided and hence, we are not the right company to work with.

As a DNA, we continue to be helpful. We understand why people say what they say. We wish them and help them move on. Emotions block people from learning and progressing.

Failures and Grievance Handling

While we do have great recruiters, interviewers, a pretty decent interview process and humane-ness and empathy in place, failures do happen. This could be because someone skipped a process, the handover from one person to another person did not happen smoothly, a certain lack of communication and visibility. All of this impacts the experience for a candidate and what impacts them certainly impacts all of us.

Irrespective of the occurrence being small, a bad experience is a bad experience. We acknowledge it when it happens. We apologize and bring in necessary course corrections to prevent the mistake from repeating.

Equally, when candidates are desperate to get their next job and are told that they don't fit the role, they get very emotional about it and even at times write bad stuff about their experience with Moolya interviewing experience. The way we take it is not personal. Of course, we do investigate to see if we missed something but if the candidate was happy throughout and became upset because there was a No Fitment, we understand their emotions.

If they rant about it publicly, we provide a polite response and offer any other help they may require. It really doesn't help them immediately but after a month or so they realize that they were treated well in Moolya. We understand it totally. We win over people in the long term. Not by showing them they are wrong or we are right. We are okay to be right but seen as wrong and win people in the long term.

Placement

M.S. Dhoni, ex-captain of the Indian cricket team is a great hitter and unleashes his power playing at position 5. Jonty Rhodes, ex-player of the South African cricket team, super famous for his fielding acrobatics is usually placed at the gully position.

Why?

The biggest mistake most talented people make is they think because of their talent - they need to be in positions 1 and 2. Many leaders also get their most talented people to open an inning (metaphorically) and lose them out early.

Even talented people need to be placed in a certain position. Our placement team understands the person coming on board and positions them rightly to our customers to create massive success for Moolyan, our customers and hence for all of us in the ecosystem.

For example, in one case, our customer was making the mistake we made in our early days thinking that extroverts can only shine, introverts can't. We brought in an introvert and told our customer to go against their belief with just this one Moolyan and see after 6 months what impact it has really made. The project needed the kind of talent we brought in but none of them in the project realized it. Our placement team and leadership team did.

This person then turned out to be the customer's go-to person for some things and they thanked us a lot for helping them see beyond what they were seeing.

The placement team looks into:

- Tech factors
- Skill factors
- Project context
- Candidate background
- Suitability to the environment
- Suitability to the colleagues
- Suitability to the aspiration of the candidate
- Suitability to the criticality of the project
- Suitability to the culture of the customer
- Time to start showing value
- Learnability
- History of the customer
- Delivery team feedback
- And more

Before enabling the newly onboarded Moolyan to be a part of the project, this care and time they put in prevented plenty of misfits from getting into a project.

Failures do happen. However, strong learning and course correction have helped reduce the failures to a large extent. A successful company doesn't mean everything is perfect. It means there is a constant chase of excellence and there is never a point where we are done in certain areas.

Chapter 11

Storytelling a Hard Thing

Storytelling - A powerful influencer

Stories move the world. We all know it. The poor storytelling that many organizations and media have done about testing, quality, bugs and value from testing has actually made many people in this world look at testing as a very shallow function for growth.

Most of the marketing we see in testing talks about automation being faster than humans. We never buy a car that says, "Faster than Eliud Kipchoge." Why? It sounds absurd. Why would we compare a machine to a human? Yet, even in 2023 many automation tools are sold this way.

It is easy to belittle humans and sell a tool. That apparently is the most popular technique of marketing and sales. Now, we don't blame them. With the pressure they have, they need to come up with eye-catching statements and nothing as exciting as "This AI will replace many Testing jobs" and we all get too curious about such articles. Some of us aren't worried about AI replacing us, we are, as a matter of fact, excited about being replaced in things we don't want to do and moving closer to what we want to. The space of software and testing is expanding phenomenally in the A.I. world. Yet, even A.I. tools are marketed as a replacement for humans. The narrative sticks in people's minds.

Marketing and Sales people don't come with a Testing background and don't have the inclination to learn testing to the extent they can speak like a testing thought leader. That said, there are wonderful new generations of community builders and marketers such as Tristan Lombard who has worked in Marketing roles across Sauce Labs, Testim and Provar has shown an immense inclination to learn testing and speak things more sensible to what humans and machines can do. This is a good hope for better narratives about Testing and the value it can deliver to organizations to fuel growth.

In Moolya, we have had good leaders in Marketing who were passionate about learning about Testing and its value. They were not afraid to speak about value without catchy *click-baity* articles. Madhurnath Rao did a brilliant job of laying a foundation for Moolya Marketing. As time evolved we realized that instead of Marketing and even before Marketing, we needed a powerful storytelling team.

Rucha Jhadav, our Storytelling Head, built a wonderful team of storytellers who bring value out to this world. The key to being able to bring the stories out. Her team members partner with Leaders within Moolya and interview testers to learn insights and bring stories of value to this world.

We wanted to share some visual content they came up with that puts a good new revolution in the world of Marketing – Testing Value. What she and her team are doing can change the narrative of the value of testing from saving cost to aiding growth and bringing value across stakeholders. We hope every other Marketing team of any testing company emulates this. Moolya alone can't change this narrative but we are doing our bit.

I want to create a long list of test cases for this problem.
Do you know the context of this problem ?
Wannabe Tester
OG Tester
No.
Wannabe Tester
OG Tester

Automation
No More ManualTesters, Phew !
What !
Why ?
Noob
OG
So, Have you automated Manual Programming ?
Automation
Because it's Slow. Duh !
Noob
OG

I want to create a long list of test cases for this problem.
Do you know the context of this problem ?
Wannabe Tester
OG Tester
No.
Wannabe Tester
OG Tester

Ughh all 1 star ratings!
Did you make a comprehensive UI/UX Test Plan ?
Wannabe Tester
OG Tester
No. Why?
That's your answer. Thank me later...
Wannabe Tester
OG Tester

Many Test / Project Managers :

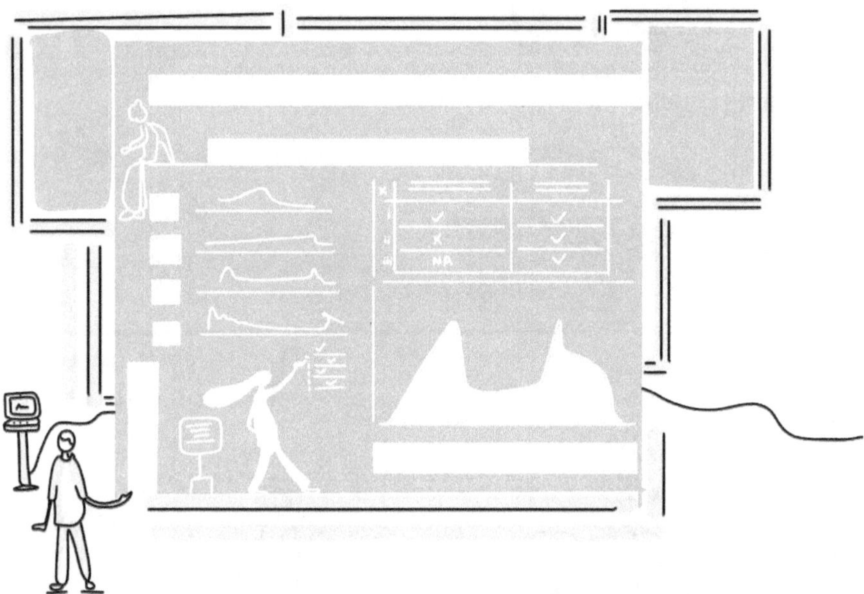

Rely on test cases when they want to provide traceability / share efforts with Stakeholders.

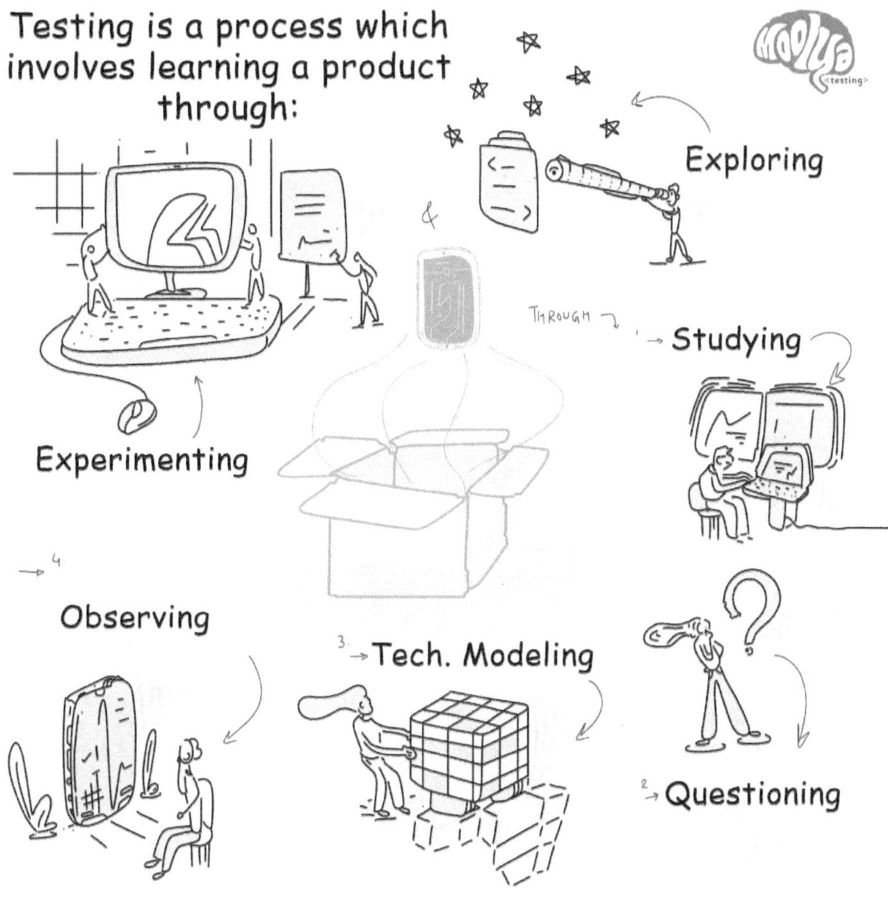
Testing is a process which involves learning a product through:
Exploring
Studying
Experimenting
THROUGH
Observing
Tech. Modeling
Questioning
moolya
<testing>

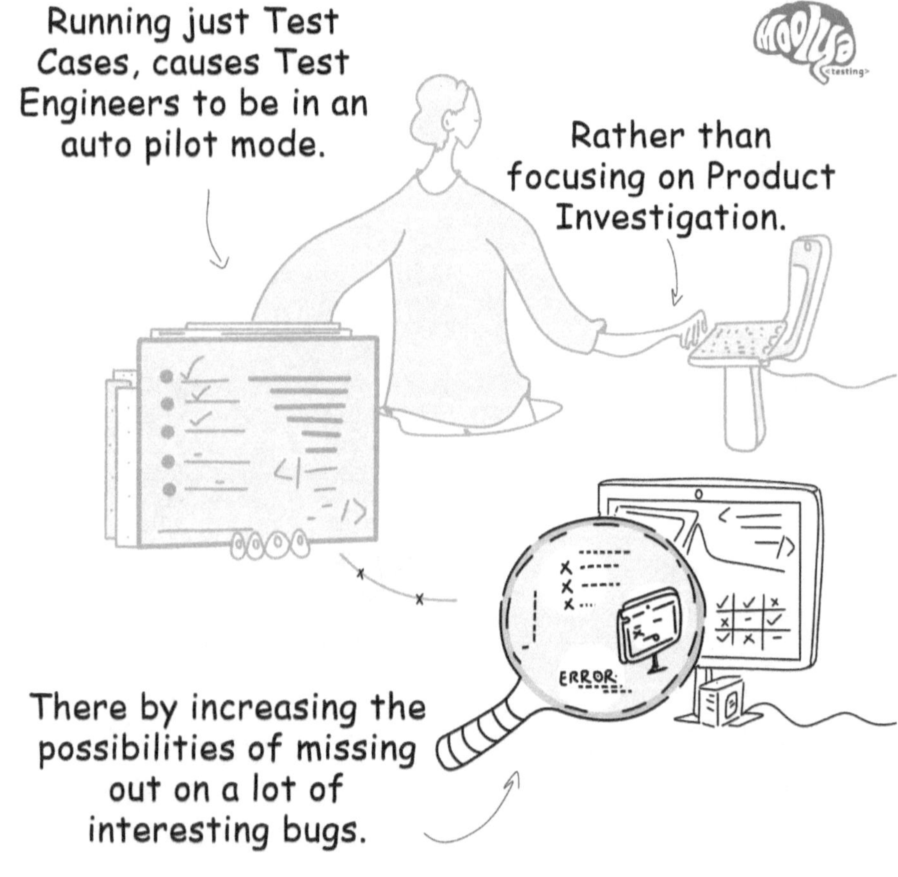
Running just Test Cases, causes Test Engineers to be in an auto pilot mode.
Rather than focusing on Product Investigation.
ERROR:
There by increasing the possibilities of missing out on a lot of interesting bugs.

Traceability is not only about providing tests mapped to the requirements.

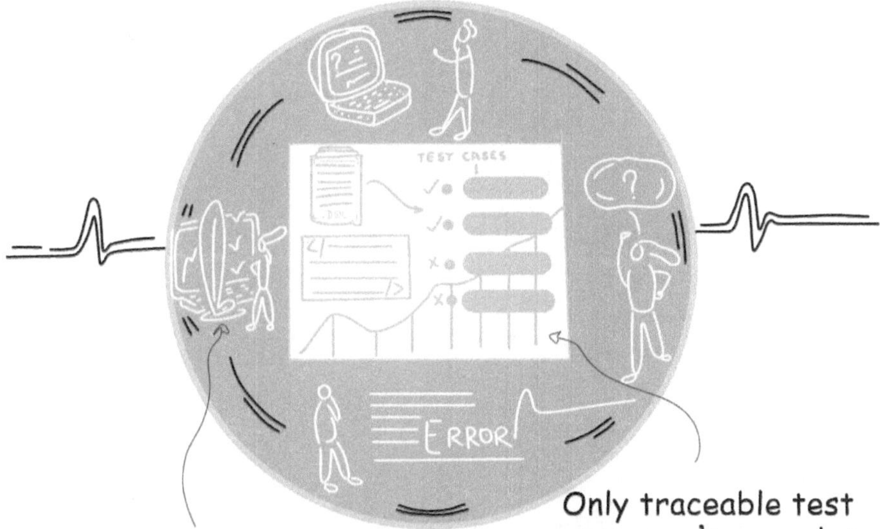

It is also about discovering and learning what the requirement documents do not mention.

Only traceable test cases aren't enough to catch all the issues.

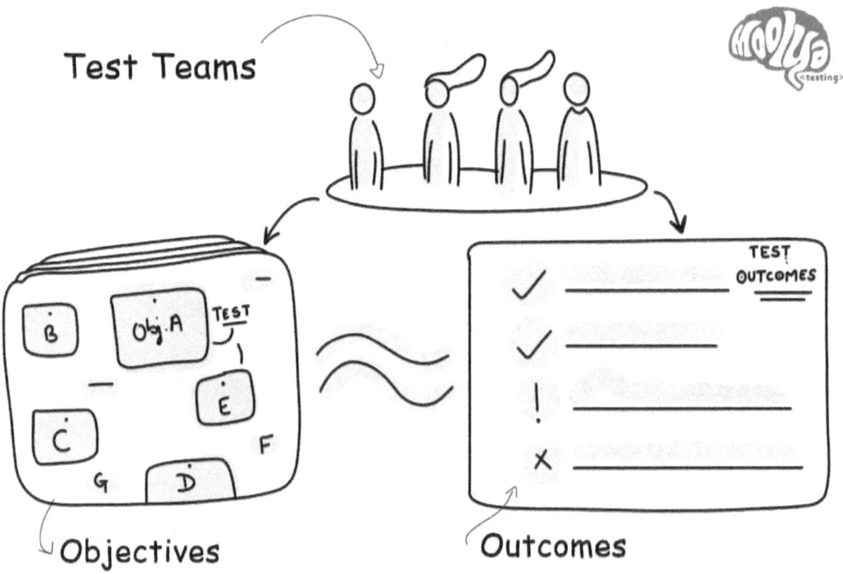

In Addition, Test teams can focus on building logical connections between the objectives of their designed tests and their outcomes.

Testing related efforts can be shared based on the phases of tests rather than adding numbers to test cases.

PHASES –

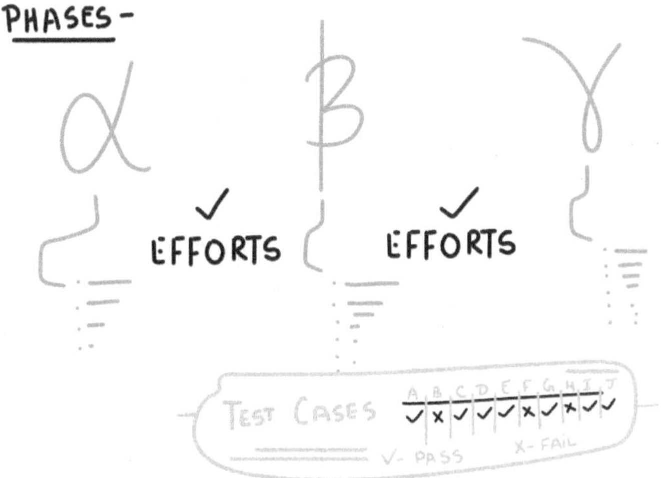

For Example,
70% of test cases passing does *not* mean that the product is functioning 70% fine.

For sharing product and feature knowledge with the newly joining Test Engineers, it's important to enable them to examine and interact with :

Product / Product Prototype.

Requirements to be analyzed

Older version of the Product

Product Standards

Competitive / Comparable Product

Marketing Claims

Contd →

CONTD
New Test Engineers should
also know about / how to :

Product
Specifications

Paired
Testing

Pairing with
a domain expert
to understand
the business
rules.

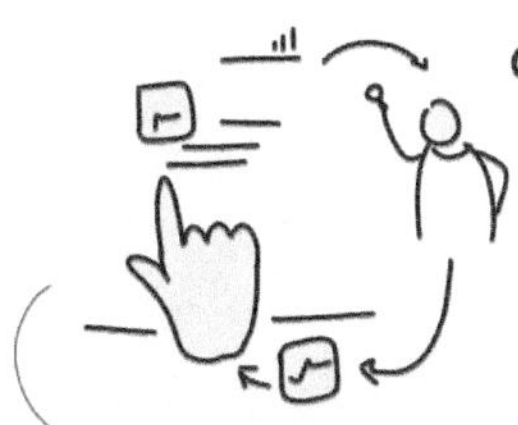
Interpret pictorial
representations of the
product.

We were recently part of a blockchain product that solves security & storage for SaaS & Businesses.

It is important to realise that, testing for apps that are built using Blockchain requires different:

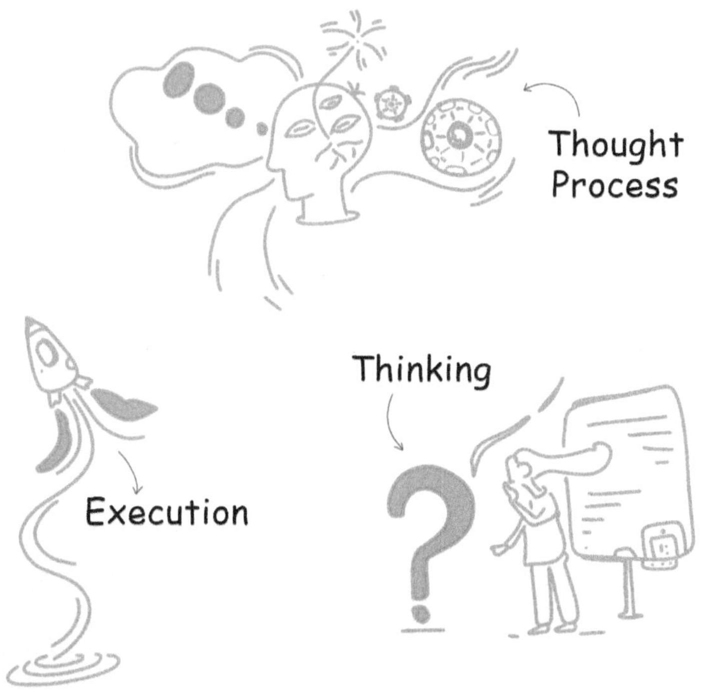

Firstly, blockchain is simply not visible. Most of the transaction happens in the back-end using ETH, Polygon, etc.

Every Blockchain has its own:

Charges

Integration Cycle

Execution Time

Update Cycle

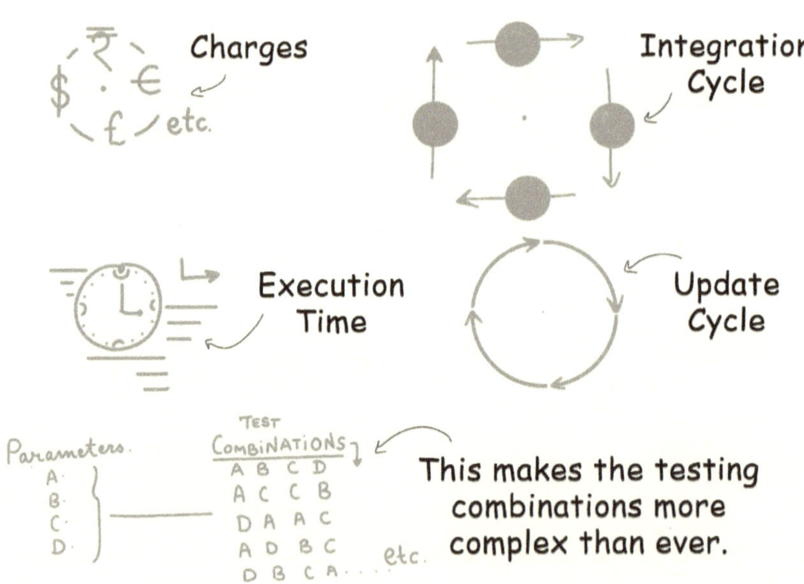

This makes the testing combinations more complex than ever.

Currently all of the products that are being built on is all new, which means:

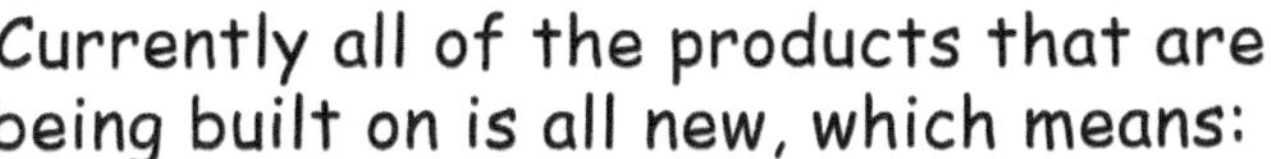

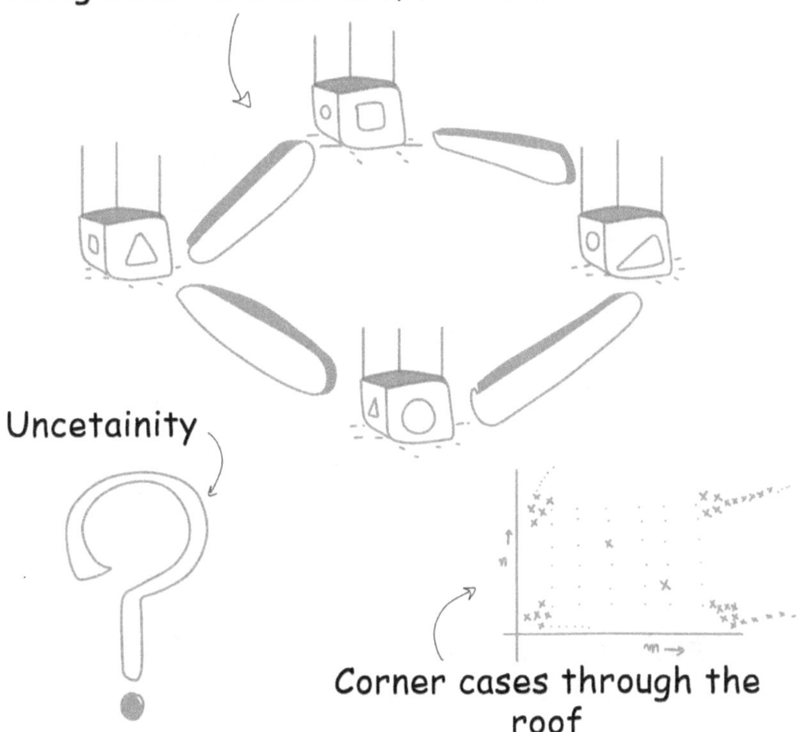

Uncetainity

Corner cases through the
roof

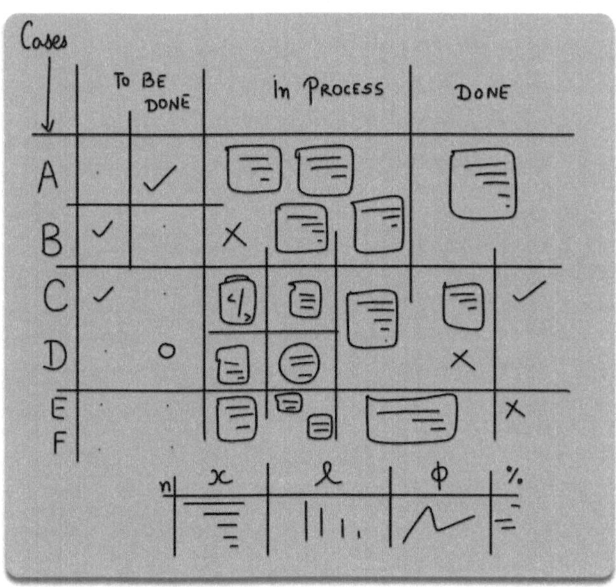

Traditional product test ideas often won't
work on apps built on blockchain.

Here is how we approached this problem:

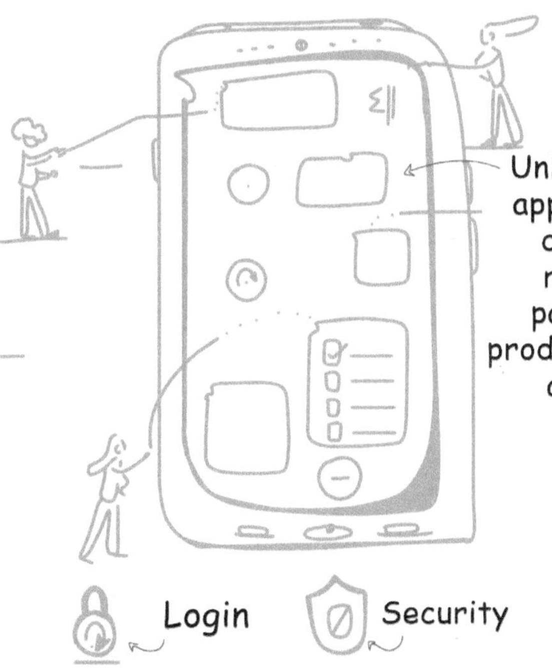

Unlike other products / apps we are testing, we don't have anything readymade for this particular blockchain product. We had to BUILD apps that includes:

 Login

Security

 Auth.

Storage

File Types

etc.

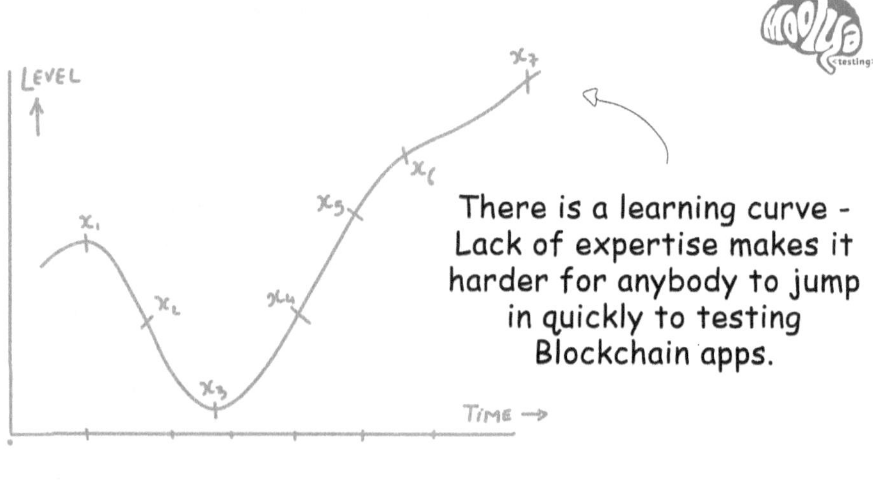

There is a learning curve - Lack of expertise makes it harder for anybody to jump in quickly to testing Blockchain apps.

Built our entire testing with APIs - This makes it easier to verify transactions much faster than UI.

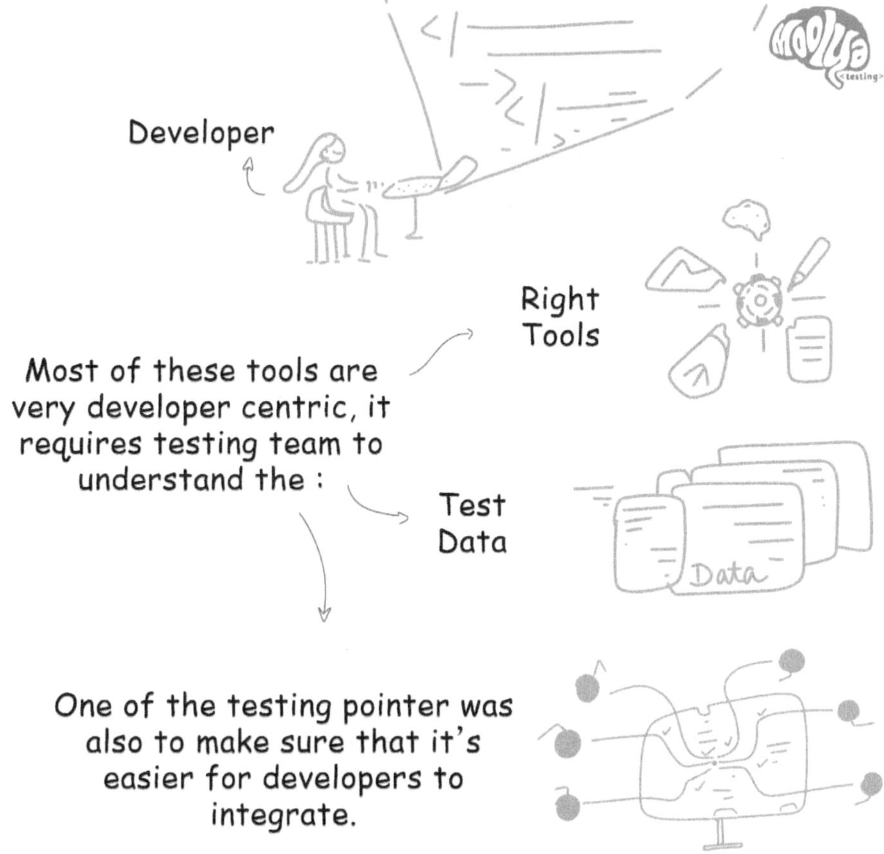

Most of these tools are very developer centric, it requires testing team to understand the :

One of the testing pointer was also to make sure that it's easier for developers to integrate.

Here are the list of tools that shall be helpful in the days to come:

- Ethereal tester -
https://github.com/ethereum/eth-tester

- Exonum -
https://exonum.com/doc/version/latest/advanced/
service-testing/

- Truffle -
https://github.com/trufflesuite/truffle

- Ganache -
https://github.com/trufflesuite/ganache-ui

More power to blockchain, more learning for the
testing community!

The World is changing in every sense.

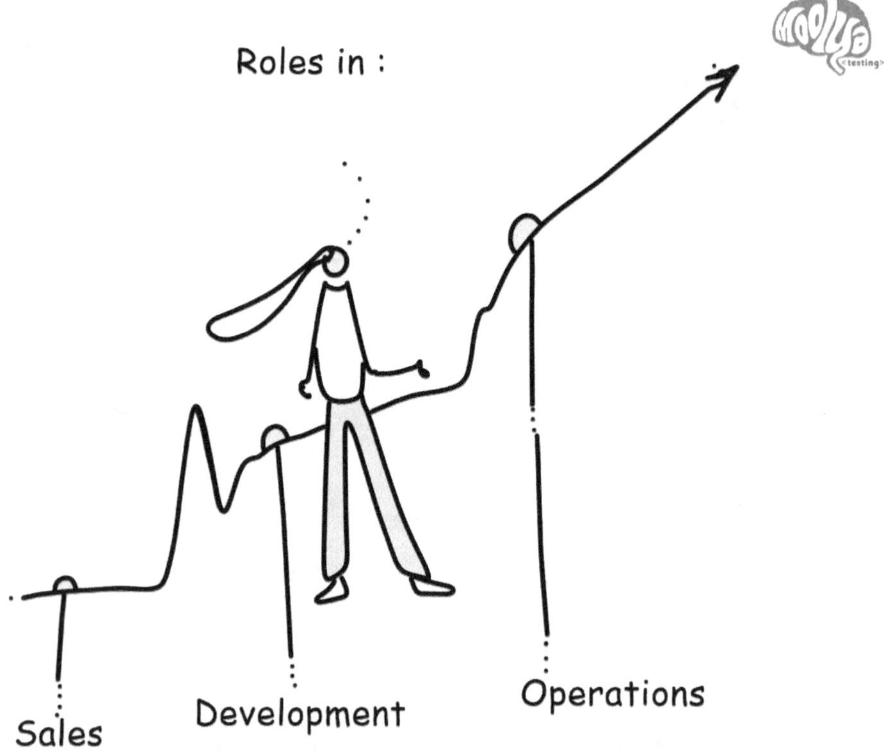

Are growing rapidly. This is a good sign.

Given this understanding and having worked and solved problems for 100s of customers.

Moolya is looking to take some huge steps towards building roles that enable people to not just grow but evolve for our customers.

We require intellectual and complex challenges
to grow, this requires for us to understand the
deeper meaning behind testing....

We focus on 3 pillars :

1. Culture

Solve with
consulting

Thought
leadership

CXO
Advisory

We focus on 3 pillars :

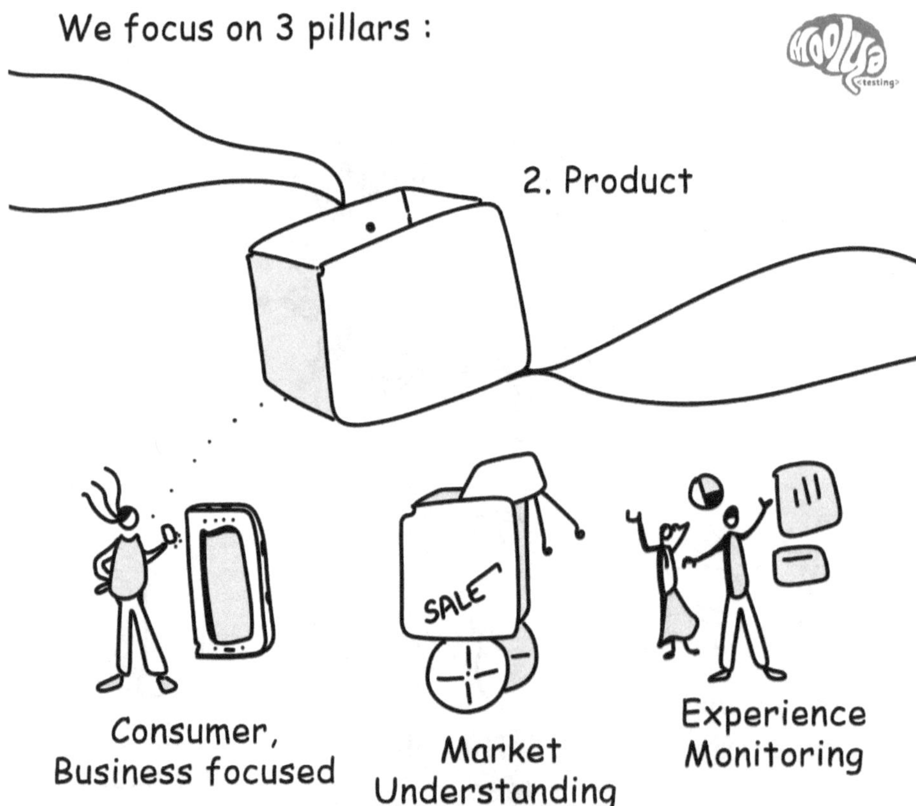

We focus on 3 pillars :

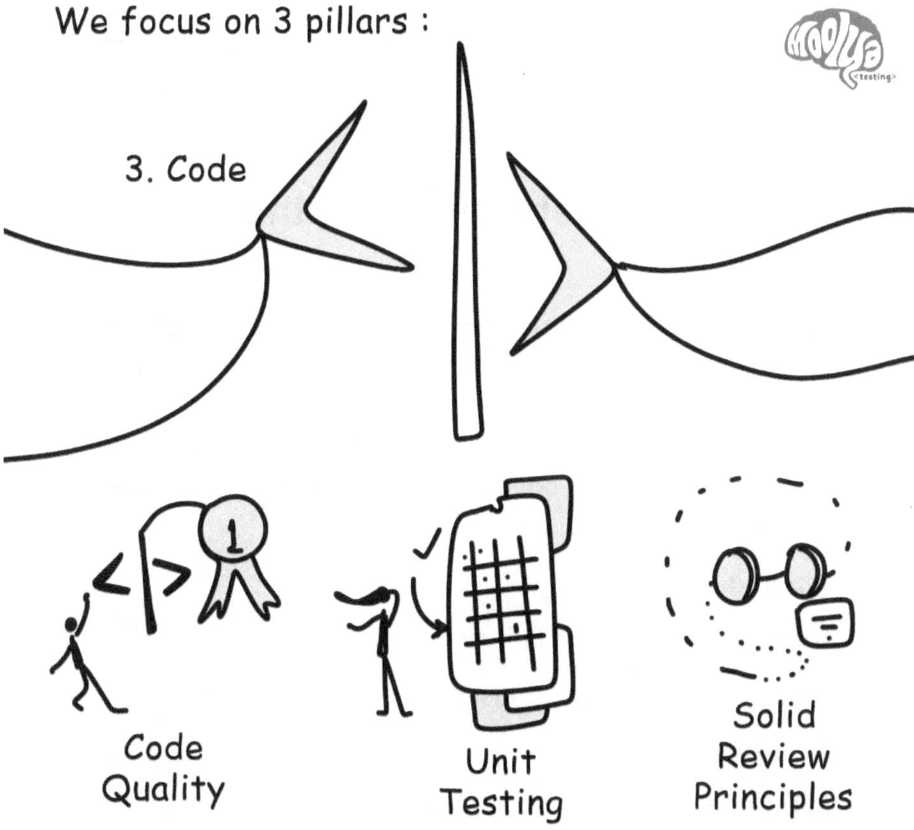

CHAPTER 12

Giving Back to the Community

We stand on the shoulders of the community

Many testing companies today stand on the shoulders of vibrant test communities, consultants and thought leaders who contribute selflessly. Moolya is no exception with one exception that we are conscious of it. The communities in the testing space have been pivotal to making Moolya happen. Moolyans have benefited and continue to benefit from many global testing communities.

Here's a partial list

- Context-driven Testing community
- Association of Software Testing
- Ministry of Testing
- SHAPE Forum
- Weekend Testing Community
- Rapid Software Testing Community
- Agile Testing community
- The Test Tribe
- The Test Chat
- Rave Test Party

- Test Automation University
- Selectors Hub community

Giving as a way of life

To give, one must multiply what was taken. The way to multiply is to give.

This is what we believe in.

We take plenty from the world and multiply it by implementing them at our work to benefit our customers and take from our customers and find ways to give back to the communities and conferences that have enriched us to add value.

When Moolya was founded, we understood the value of every payment our customers made and we were sending them flowers, every time they made a payment. As we grew, we replaced the flowers with planting a tree for every payment a customer makes to Moolya and today, we have a mini forest growing planted just out of timely payments our customers have made over the last decade.

Supporting creators and contributors

Moolya has always supported creators and contributors who are committed to helping the Test and QA community worldwide to learn, innovate and succeed. Since its inception, Moolya and most importantly Moolyans have contributed to and supported many community initiatives.

Partial list of conference speaking engagements by Moolyans:

- CAST, USA
- Start West, USA
- STPCon, USA
- TWST, Canada
- EuroStar, Europe

- QA and Test, Spain
- Copenhagen Context, Denmark
- Let's Test, Sweden
- Test Bash, UK
- Selenium Conference, India
- StepIn Summit, India
- BWST, India
- TribalQonf, India
- Test Mu, Global Online

Testing Books Moolya has bought in bulk to distribute to Moolyans:

- Explore It! - Elisabeth Hendrickson
- Lessons Learned in Software Testing - Cem Kaner, James Bach, Bret Pettichord
- Buddha in Testing - Pradeep Soundararajan
- Perfect Software and Other Illusions About Testing - Gerald M Weinberg

Moolya brings the community together through 2 conferences

- MITC: Moolya Internal Testing Conference
- TestEd: A public conference for the betterment of the craft of testing

Deep thinking and testing competition hosted by Moolya

- Moolympics
  - Preventing bugs
  - Selectors
  - Coaching Testers
  - Mindmapping

MoolyaEd community activities

- Podcast hosted by Amit Vyas

- Fresher training at Universities: 1000+ engineering graduates touched every year

- Partnerships with universities to bring practical software testing training thought process to pre-final and final year engineering students

Bugasura Bytes

- Bringing entrepreneurs building AI products together

- Creating opportunities for Testers and Developers to interact with Entrepreneurs in the AI space

Apart from this,

- Moolya offices are open for any testing community work on weekends

- Moolya set up a public library (pre covid) for any non-Moolyan to also access any tech and testing books available in Moolya.

- Moolyans have tutorials on testing and automation shared over Moolya's YouTube channel.

- Moolyans are open to coaching passionate testers.

- Moolyans have participated in and won many testing competitions.

Why is this chapter in this book?

In the busy world of taking, a reminder always helps that the purpose of taking is to give back. Moolya has had a culture of giving that creates a high density of testers who give.

A lot of young or newbie testers think, "What do I have to give?" or "I am not yet an expert, to give." This thought process comes from low self-confidence. Volunteering at a non-profit conference registration desk is a way to give, to start with. Participating in meetups is a way to lay the foundation to give. Organizing and supporting such initiatives gives exposure to givers. Surrounding ourselves with givers is also what makes us givers. If we keep denying ourselves the opportunity to be around givers, we will never become one.

Being a Moolyan, it is important to know the DNA of being a Moolyan means to become a giver. Giving is a way of our living. Give to people who shall further the craft.

CHAPTER **13**

The Proof is Always in the Pudding

When Moolya was founded, the idea that testing being a direct influence and impact on customer, revenue and profitability growth was theoretical. Every other organization claimed they are good in domain knowledge, good in reducing manual effort (sigh), good in automation, and good in a cost-efficient way to test but literally no one who said, "We will be the growth engine for you." Maybe they indirectly did but not consciously.

There was no single largest organization that did it as a focus. Moolya is the largest scale experiment that delivered the results for a growth-driven approach to testing. We also hope there will be more and we could become their students and learn from them.

Last week, one of our existing customers, Manoj Kumar, CTO of Avysh referred us to another customer (and we acquire 90% of our new customer base through referrals) and the following is what he wrote on his own:

Manoj Kumar avysh.com>
to abha.

Hello /

Hope you are doing good. I would like to introduce our partner company Moolya to you. They can be a very fruitful partner for your companies.

Few months ago we realized that there is a certain nagging issue impacting our business. It was only after talking with the folks at Moolya we were able to figure out what it was. Then together we fixed it.

Like many enterprises we had a very generic idea about the impact of testing when it comes to business. That perception changed completely when we started our relationship with Moolya.

Let us tell you why exactly:
- Moolya has this unique knack of looking at things from the customer's perspective.
- They practically co-own the project with their customers
- They believe that the majority of the problems lie within the culture of an organization and hence they aim to fix it together.
- They have extensive experience in working with C-level, V-level, and D-level executives thereby bringing in holistic changes in technology, business, and culture
- Their focus is not just on fixing the immediate problems but also deliver large scale transformation programs

Why should you trust Moolya with your business and culture?
- They've catered to 200+ clients
- Covering 20 countries
- With a journey of more than 12 years now
- Brands like Flipkart, Swiggy, PayTM, PhonePe, Myntra have entrusted Moolya with their testing and business solutions
- And so did we

If you have a hunch that there's a persistent problem with your digital product or you feel that it's not reaching its true potential then schedule a call with Moolya.

Manoj and many other CTOs, CEOs, CPOs, VP Engineering, and Expert Consultants have vouched for us because the value from testing they have seen is a growth-driven testing approach to the products and business they were building. They love our obsession with customer growth. It makes businesses successful. Otherwise, we wouldn't be standing strong at 12 years!

Can this only be done in Moolya?

We could use another example from our own customer but what better validation than another large services company acknowledging how Moolya Way of Testing is changing their game with their customer?

Persistent Systems, a 1 Billion USD enterprise that has a legacy of working with large enterprises, put this award out to Mohanraj Paneerselvam, who took Moolya's approach of testing and implemented it in the project he was working on.

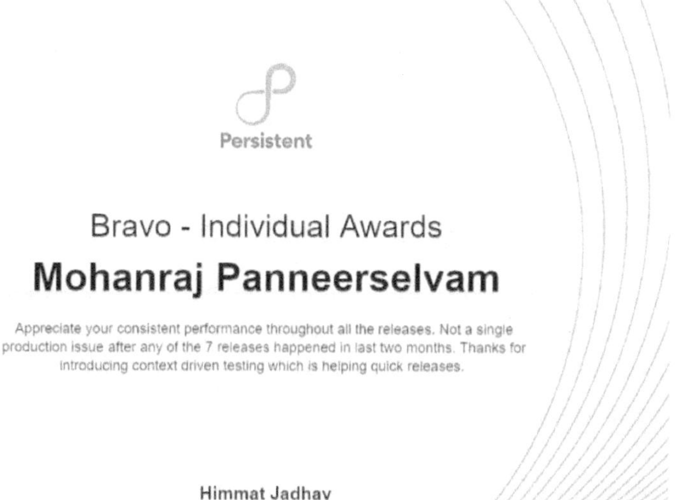

The award says, "Not a single production bug in the last 7 releases." Moolya's tagline is preventing bugs and we keep sensitizing our people to prevent bugs and not just find bugs. Testers don't understand business and business stakeholders. They understand bugs. Translating a vision to reality only happens when people on the ground can create an impact.

We congratulate Mohanraj and Persistent for achieving this feat together. Mohanraj took to Linkedin to express his kindness and credit Moolya for helping him learn this approach which made this achievement possible. It is certainly his kindness and his work and that of his whole team to make it happen but we are fortunate to have played an incidental role in making this happen. We are celebrating their win. Why? It is a win for all testers. The new bar set for other testers to catch up to is to prevent bugs. This is a good thing for the world. This is good for everyone: CEOs, CTOs, CPOs, VPs, Directors, Managers, Leads, Engineers and most importantly, Customers and end users.

We want to spread the mindset of testing driving growth in this world. The world has to come together to make this happen. This book is an attempt to open source how we function in Moolya so that it becomes possible for other teams across the globe to take the good parts and build their test teams to be growth savvy and build true growth for their stakeholders and customers.

The future is growth-driven

We strongly believe that when startups and enterprises taste a faster, cleaner, more efficient way to serve customers and grow their topline and bottom line, it is hard for them to let go of the approach in favour of old and addictive bad practices in testing. Equally, our understanding is – if we had not figured this out and executed it at the scale we executed – someone else would have. The world is not waiting for anyone. It is moving at a fast pace. Those who build growth for others - grow. Those who don't are made redundant.

The only test all test teams in the world have to pass is – whatever they are doing – is it resulting in growth? If this test fails and all other tests pass, the value of testing is a fail. As Moolya, we are happy to support any team within and outside of Moolya to drive growth for their stakeholders and customers.

You have reached a new beginning!

Gratitude to Mr Sriram Tadimalla for the guidance to Moolya as a mentor. Thanks to Sunil Kumar and Parimala Hariprasad, who believed in us in the early days of the journey. Thanks to Bhavana Vasudev, Esha Medha and Robert Sabourin for helping us by offering improvements that have enabled us to bring this book to you in this shape. Special thanks to Himanshu Gopalani for the cover design of this book.

The material presented here is a combination of many Moolyans coming together. As a token of expressing our true gratitude for all those who made it possible to present this book to you, we would like to print their names. These are the people who made Moolya possible. We have done our best to collect all names since the inception of Moolya and any misses in this list are unintentional.

A Harsha Vardhan, Aakash Gupta, Aarathy Sidappreddy, Aarti Kumari, Abhas Sinha, Abhay A Kotwal, Abhijeet Kumar, Abhijeet Rajpurohit, Abhijeet Saxena, Abhijith Shetty, Abhilash T, Abhilash Toofran, Abhishek, Abhishek Chauhan, Abhishek Eknath Kadam, Abhishek Ghildiyal, Abhishek Gupta, Abhishek Kumar, Abhishek Mohan N, Abhishek Purohit, Abhishek Raj, Abhishek Singh, Abilash N, Acsah Mathew, Adhithya Prahladh V, Adhithya Sankar, Adil Imroz, Adithya Ajith, Aditi Agrawal, Aditi Mahendra Rajarshi, Aditi P Bellur, Aditya, Aditya Acharya, Aditya Gaurav, Afreen, Aishurya Sahoo, Aishwarya Gautam Salve, Aishwarya John, Ajay Kumar Singh, Ajay Mohan, Ajison Edattu, Akanksha Dama, Akanksha Kriti, Akanksha Sinha, Akarsh Sahu, Akash Bera, Akash Tiwari, Akhil S Nair, Akhil Viswanathan, Akhilesh Kumar Singh, Akramul Hussain Barbhuiya, Akshata Indaragi, Akshata Jeevendrappa Indaragi, Akshata Vinod, Akshatha A Kumar, Akshatha B A, Akshatha Km, Akshay Ashok, Akshay Patil, Akshaya Singh, Alan Jose, Alapati Vasavi, Alekha Swain, Ali Mandal, Allaka Ravi Kumar, Alok Kumar Pandey, Alpesh Chhaganlal Dana, Amal K Saji, Aman Anand, Aman Sharma, Amba Jha, Ameet Kumar Pradhan, Amit Vyas, Ammireddy Vandana, Amol Mishra, Amrita Kumari, Amrutha R, Amudha R, Amudha.r, Amulya Poojary, Anamika Singh, Anand Iyer, Anant Dubey, Ananya Ranganath, Anbarasu S, Anil Kumar Tank, Anish Kumar, Anitha B V, Anjali Kumari Jha, Ankesh Bhutada, Ankit Singh Yadav, Ankita Vyas, Ankitha P A Upadhya, Ankur Bharti, Ankur Jain, Annashree L, Annashree Lakshmeesh, Annavarapu Naga Venkata Yaswanth Kumar, Anshul Agrawal, Anshul Soni, Antima Yadav, Anu A Nambiar, Anu M P, Anuj Mishra, Anupam Kalita, Anupam Saurabh, Anurag Arora, Anurag Bharti, Anurag Khode, Anusha Manikchand Desai, Anusha Rao, Anushree V, Anwesha Guha Roy, Apeksha Hunagund, Arati Ajit Kote, Arati Suresh Chavan, Aravind Muthukrishnan, Aravindanath D M, Arigarla Jayakala, Arjeet Banchhor, Arjun P, Arjun Pol, Arjun Pujar, Arjun R, Arjun Ravi, Arko Chakraborty, Arpita, Arpita Majumdar, Arpitha K.b, Arsha Mohan, Arthy. C, Arun Kumaar T S, Arun V, Arushree Vyas, Arvind Kumar, Aryan Sharma,

Asfiya Sultana, Asha C Kharat, Ashirbad Patra, Ashish Kumar, Ashok K, Ashok Kumar Gokinapalli, Ashok Prabhu, Ashok Prabhu Thanikasalam, Ashwani Kumar, Ashwath Kumar, Ashwin B A, Ashwin B.a., Ashwini L, Ashwini Raj, Astha Jain, Asutosh Mishra, Aswin Suri, Athira V L, Avinash Baradabadi, Avinash Joshuva Nishant, Avinash Ks, Aviral Gupta, Ayush Jadon, Ayush Mandloi, Ayush Singh Chauhan, B Geetika Subudhi, B Sandiyaa, B Sivakesava, Balasubramanian Kanthasamy, Balasubramanyam M V, Balisha, Banoth Sushmith Naik, Barathraman R, Basavarajesh Koni, Basil Sunny, Bhakti Karale, Bhanuprakash Cn, Bharanidharan R, Bharat Chitara, Bharati J Naik, Bhaskar, Bhaskar Varma Penmethsa, Bhavana Mutha G, Bhavana V, Bhavana Vasudeva, Bhavani Kumari, Bhavani Tharun, Bhavya Srivastava, Bhavya Swaroop, Bheemesha N, Bhimesh Bittu, Bhimraj Gupta, Bhuvaneshwari, Bikash Kumar, Bindiya N, Bindu A S, Binutha B R, Bittu Kumar, Boopathy Rajendran, Brajesh Mishra, Brajesh Purohit, Brindha Kandhasamy, Bukkala Suneel Kumar, Bushra Fathima, Chaitra H, Chalapathi Rao Gondi, Chandan Kumar, Chandan Kumar Nayak, Chandan Kumar Saha, Chandini Mokthar, Chandrakumar H S, Chethan K, Chethan Ramesh, Chethan Sanjay, Chhaya Dilip Pawar, Chidambara M R, Chidambaram Ganesan, Chiraag Ps, Chirag Mittal, Chitanya Kanavi, Chitranshi Chopra, D Jaswanth Kumar, D Monishree, Damayanti Chowdhury, Damini Gandhe, Darpan Ganesh Shet, Darshan C, Darshan Joshi, Darshani, Deepa Bhat, Deepak B.p, Deepak Sekar, Deepak Tiwari, Deepali Patil, Deepika M, Deepthi P Rao, Defney Sneha Lobo, Dev Karan Punia, Dev M M, Devendra Kumar Deshmukh, Devi R, Devika, Dey Kumar, Dhanalakshmi Bc, Dhanasekar S, Dhanashree Ashok Bhosale, Dharmalingam K, Dhiraj Bothra, Dikjyoti Phukan, Dikshant Dixit, Dikshita Basumatary, Dilip Kumararaj G, Dimple Kumari, Dinesh Kumar, Dinesh L, Disha Agarwal, Divya G, Divya Srivastava, Divya Tripathi, Divya V Narendra, Divya.g, E Ganesh, Edward Wilson S, Eesha Rajendra Borkar, Erumbala Shwetha Nambiar, Esha Meda Ganesh, Esha Sinha, Eshan Dhanpal, Ezhilarasan E, Ezhilarasu Johnson. J, Gagan D Shetty, Gagan Kv, Gagan R, Gangesh Chennapa, Ganpal Ramanjaneya Reddy, Gaurabh Chakraborty, Gaurav Kumar, Gautam K R, Gautam M S, Gautam Mududy Sureshababu, Gautham Sk, Gayathri S, Gayathri Seenivasan, Gayatri M, Geetha S, Geethanjali R, Gokhul Salgun, Gokul Gn, Gokul Venugopal, Gokula Krishnan, Gopal Ram Choudhary, Goutham D A, Goutham Kanade, Gowtham V, Gurinder Singh, Gurjeet Singh, Gurudevi S, Haarika K, Hadasa Tenneti,

Hamsa Nandini, Hari Krishna Recharla, Hari Krishnan, Hariharaman M, Harikrishnan D, Harish G, Harish S, Harish Soodi, Harsha Kulkarni, Harsha Teja, Harshal Chaudhari, Harshal P, Harshita A J, Harshita G, Harshita Nathawat, Harshitha Aj, Harshitha Gowda, Himadri Sengupta, Himadri Thanki, Himansha Tyagi, Himanshu Gopalani, Himanshu Tak, Himansu Senapati, Hina P Shah, Hitesh Kumar Patel, Hithashree V, Indhumathi Balakrishnan, Indu Shrimantrao Biradar, Irfan Haneef, Irfan Shariff, Isha Malik, Ishrath Fatima, Ishrath Fatima Shaik, Ishwarya B.s, Jahnavi B, Jameel Rizwan, Janani Kumaresan, Jaswant R, Jayachandra Reddy Vattem, Jayanth G, Jayanth R, Jayasree V, Jeevan V, Jens Ola Marten Hauser, Jhansi Vunnam, Jilagam Jeevan Ravi Kumar, Jisha M George, Jishnu P V, Jithendra Kumar R, John Belinda Ann, Johnson E, Juhi Kumari, Jyothi R, Jyoti Singh Gour, Jyoti Vagukar, K H Shiva Kumar, K V Nandan, K.pranitha Devaiah, Kadiyam Vijayarchana, Kalpana A Kembavi, Kalpita Mishra, Kalyan Chandrapu, Kamini Acharya, Kamleshkumari Choudhary, Kanav Raina, Kanchan Galar, Kannan Chidambaram, Kantepalli Sai Sasanka, Karan Singh, Karanam Dheeraj, Karna Prasanth Reddy, Karthik D.n, Karthik H.p, Kartik S Kulkarni, Kaul Ramit Manohar, Kaviarasu Palanisamy, Kavita S, Kavitha Rao, Kavitha U, Kavya D, Kavya G S, Kazim Farid, Kedar Suhas Kulkarni, Keerthi Prabhu, Ken D'silva, Ken Dsilva, Kenguva Geetha Madhuri, Ketan Chandra, Khalid Dalwale, Khazal Ammaarah, Kiran Ankappa, Kiran Magadum, Kirthi Kumar, Kiruthika Arunachalam, Kishor Br, Kishor Jogannavar, Kokonda Nikhil Kumar, Krati Vyas, Kripa S, Krishan Raj Borana, Krishna K, Krishna Rajendran, Krishnamurthy S G, Krishnaveni Kunda, Krishnendu Halder, Krithika M N, Kruthika G Hegde, Kshitij Hastu, Kshitiz Srivastava, Kumar Saurabh, Kumar Suryanshu, Kunal , Kunal Gehlot, Kuravati Rajesh, Kuravati Ramesh, Kushal M, Kusum Lata Narzary, Kusuma S, Lakshay Bhati, Lakshmi Prasanna, Lalitha Bettadapura, Lata Ganesh Naik, Lathesh Ps, Lavanya N, Lawrence Fernandes, Laxmikant S Murkute, Lenssen S, Liesl Vincent Vellara, Lijo George, Likhith H Jain, Lipika Das, Lisa Das, Logesh Prabhu, M Nikhil Goud, M V Manoj, M. harsha Teja, Madan Kumar A S, Madeline Faustina, Madhavan Srinivasan, Madhukeshwara B, Madhura S Bhatt, Madhuri Gopinath, Madhuri H A, Madhuri N, Madhushankar D N, Madhushankar Dn, Maha Sivalingam, Mahaboob Peer, Mahalakshmi P, Mahesh K Badiger, Mahesh P, Mahesh P R, Malathi Dhandapani, Malireddy Vamsikrishna, Malkeet Singh, Mallapu Sobhitha, Mallikarjun A B, Mamatha K, Mampi Das, Mamtha Mala

Ramasamy, Manasa M, Mangesh D Nagdeve, Mani Goel, Mani Krishna, Manikandan M G, Manikaran Singh, Manish Kumar, Manish Kumar Chand, Manisha Panda, Manju M, Manju Maheswar, Manjula Hesaraghatta Lakshmaiah, Manjula Lakshmaiah, Manjunath B Narayanappa, Manjunath Krishna Naik, Manjunath S, Manohara N, Manoj M Sappan, Manoj Shirsat, Mansi Harish, Manvi Choumal, Mariya Sajan, Masoome Fatima, Mathurthi Naga Veeravenkata Brahmam, Maulik Srivastava, Md Sahil Raza, Medhashree Munipalli Padmanabh, Meenakshi Deshwal, Meenakshi Poddar, Meenambigai Ramakrishnan, Megha J, Megha Melgiri, Megha Ramprasad, Megha Singh, Meghana Jadav, Meghana K.b, Meghana K J, Meghana Sudhindra, Mehlaqua Perveen, Merlyn Nikitha Oomen, Miriyampalli Koteswari, Mithun C, Mithun Chandrashekar, Mithun S Nair, Mohamed Musthafa Gudubai, Mohamed Shakeeb Abdulla, Mohammed Arbaaz, Mohammed Irfan, Mohammed Khurram, Mohammed Shahid, Mohammed Shayaan Junaidi, Mohammed Soudagar, Mohan Basavaiah, Mohan Pattar, Mohan Ram M, Mohan Thevar M, Mohanraj Panneerselvam, Monica Movva, Monika R, Monika Rani, Monisha M, Moorthi Rajendiran, Movva Monica, Mrigakshi Sarma, Mrinalini, Mubeena B Afreen, Muhammed Favaz, Muppidi Manisha Sree, Murthy Srinivas Narasimha, Mythily Vijaykumar, Naga Dinesh Veerapu, Nagalakshmi Mn, Nagasahas Ds, Nagashree D Kumar, Nahida Parveen, Nain Tara Yadav, Nalini M P, Namrata Soni, Nandagopal Rajagopal, Nandan Shripad Pujar, Nandini V, Nannapaneni Radha, Naresh Kumaar, Naresh M, Naresh Madana, Nargis Sultana Sultana, Navadeep Chalasani, Naveen Kumar B, Navya R, Navyashree G, Navyashree K R, Nayana Hugar, Nayana K, Neerajkumar Bipinchandra Lad, Neethu Antony, Neha Jain, Neha Khare, Neha Kutten, Neha Prakash Kankure, Neha Rani, Neha Sethi, Nevuri Raji Reddy, Nidhi Upadhyay, Nidhi Verma, Nikhitha Ravi, Nikitha C, Nilesh Kumar Gupta, Niraj Kumar Gupta, Nischitha Shivanna, Nisha Gopinath Menon, Nisha Kumari, Nishant Gohel, Nishantha C K, Nitesh Goyal, Nitesh Kumar Chaubey, Nitesh Raaz, Nithin H S, Nitish Bharadwaj R, Nitish Kumar Yadav, Niveditha Narendran, Nivethan Radhakrishnan, Nomit Vyas, Oleti Akhil, Onkar N, Oviya S, P Anil Kumar, P K Harikesava Rao, P Sreenivasulu, P Usha Vani, P.sneha, Padmashree J, Palagiri Gurivi Reddy, Palakil S Visweswaran, Palavallareddy Madan, Pallavi Jadhav, Pallavi Shrishail Karbhari, Panchami B, Pandya Rahul Rajeshbhai, Pankaj Bhatia, Pankaj Kumar, Parag Kiritkumar Panchal, Parimala Hariprasad, Patan Aleem

Khan, Pathan Ayaan, Pathik Ranjan Mitra, Pavan Kumar Bojja, Pavan Kumar G, Pavan Kumar M, Perumalla Madhavi, Pooja B N, Pooja Kumari, Pooja Parasharam Maluche, Pooja S Modani, Poojarani, Poornima S Mogera, Prabhjot Singh, Pradeep, Pradeep Isreal, Pradeep Kumar N R, Pradeep Nain, Pradeepraj M, Pragati, Pragati Rai, Pragati Yadav, Prajyot P Kulkarni, Pranay Reddy S, Pranshu Shukla, Prantik Barua, Prapulla C, Prapulla Chandrasekar, Prasad Dattatraya Chorge, Prasanna Kumar, Prashant Baswaraj, Prashant Shinde, Prashanth A Bhosale, Prateek M, Prateek Mathur, Prateek Shrivastava, Prateek Vashishth, Prathiba Lakshmaiah, Prathija J Etagi, Prathima C, Pratik Thapa, Pratima Verma, Pratisha Priti Nath, Pratyush Kumar Singh, Pravada Patil, Praveen Borawar, Praveen C, Praveen Kumar N, Praveenkumar Gk, Preetham C A, Preethi D, Preethi Rachel Daniel, Premangsu Bhattacharya, Prithvi R, Priti Kumari, Priti Trivedi, Priya B, Priya Bansal, Priya Singh, Priyadarshini Ram Kumar, Priyanka Dattatray Jadhav, Priyanka M, Priyanshi Rankitbhai Thakkar, Protyusha Saha, Puligandla Bhanusagar, Pullalarevu Amarnath Reddy, Pundaleek B Handaragal, Puneet Bohra, Puneeth Jayaram, Pushpa B.c, Pushpa K, Raahul N, Rachana Lokesh, Rachana Mn, Rachana S, Radha Nannapaneni, Radhika Dhankechaya, Radhika Naresh Revankar, Radhika Sahi, Ragavi J, Raghavendra Radhakrishnan, Rahul Kumar, Rahul R K, Rahul Satish Varade, Rahul Saxena, Rahul Sharma, Raj Purkayastha, Raja Kaushik, Raja Rajeswari S, Rajarshi Gosh, Rajat Arora, Rajesh Chandra Yadav, Rajiv Ranjan Jha, Rajorshi Ghosh, Rajput Shaileshkumar Rameshwarsingh, Rakesh Kumar, Rakesh Kumar Gupta, Rakesh Madanlal Chaudhari, Rakesh P Barhate, Rakeshgouda S Patil, Rakshith R V, Rakshitha R, Ram Bohra, Ram Kiran B, Ram Konijeti, Ram Prasad N, Rama Krishna Vamsi Vasireddi, Ramavathu Prasanna Naik, Rameshwari Tukaram Chavan, Ramigani Ramakrishnareddy, Ramit Manohar, Ramya Bn, Ramya R Kulkarni, Ranbirkaur Sandhu, Ranjith K R, Ranjitha C S, Rapti Gupta, Rashi T, Rashika Koul, Rashmi P, Rashmi P N, Rashmi Shindhe, Rasmiranjan Nath, Ravichandra Hb, Ravisuriya, Reddy Prasad S, Reshma Akkali, Reshma M, Revanasiddappa Pujeri, Richa Sinha, Rishikesh Kumar Choudhary, Ritesh Jha, Ritesh R Nayak, Rithvik Bhat, Ritika Singh, Riya Chhabra, Riya Garg, Riyaj Shaikh, Robin Nagar, Roheen Ghosh, Rohini S, Rohit Grover, Rohit Tambe, Roja Kushali Gunagi, Ronak Mathur, Roopitha P, Roshni Mathankar, Roshni Ramesh, Rucha Jadhav, Ruchika Sancheti, Rudresh Joshi, Rudro Choudhury, Rukhiya Khanum, Rupali Basappa Umagol, S R Srinath, Sabareshkumar Janakiraman, Sachin G,

Sadhna Seervi, Sadiya Anwari, Sagar Kumar, Sagar Raravi, Sagarika Thareja, Sahana K, Sahil Sanskar Jha, Saiyed Sajid Ali, Saksham Dinesh Agrawal, Sakshi Singhal, Sakshi Thanvi, Samarendra Dhar, Samarth Rajesh Bagul, Samarth S, Sambit Roy, Sameena Taj, Samikshya Pattanaik, Samir Kumar Mohanty, Samved Hegde, Samyuktha N S, Sana Khursheed, Sandeep Baligeri, Sandeep Kumar Sharma, Sandeep Reddy, Sandeep Surendran, Sandhya Chaudhary, Sandhya Ramesh, Sandipan Roy, Sandra M.r, Sangeetha M, Sangili Vijay, Sanjana Hunasikatti, Sanjana Sd, Sanjay M B, Sanooj Mp, Santhosh R, Santhoshi Guggul, Santhoshkumar Mahadevan, Santoshkumar Sindagi, Santhosh Shivanand Tuppad, Sarala Kolhe, Saraswati Panda, Saravanakumar V, Sarika S Bagi, Sarita Mohapatra, Sashank Koundinya, Sastha Prabhu T, Satabdi Roy, Satyam Dixit, Saurabh Bhura, Saurabh Chakraborty, Saurabh Chaudhary, Saurabh Ghildiyal, Saurabh Gupta, Saurav Kumar Pati, Saurish Dutta, Sayantani Goswami, Selvamani Ramanathan, Shabnam K, Shah Yagnesh Harshadbhai, Shaik Kasmoormastanvali, Shaik Mukhaddar, Shalini J, Shalini Katari, Shanawaz Usman Mansuri, Shanmugam Moorthy, Shantaveeresh B, Sharan K Kumar, Sharan Kumar M, Sharanabasappa Channappa Doddameti, Sharath B R, Shareef Shaik, Sharika Ahmed, Sharvari Belliappa, Shashank Jain, Shashi Kumar N, Sheetal Vijay Kakati, Shefali Shrivastava, Sheril Francis, Shesha Rajendra Borkar, Shibangi Panda, Shibani Kumar, Shilpa Lingaraddi, Shiv Prassad, Shivadhara, Shivam Singh, Shivam Tyagi, Shivanagouda Madnalli, Shivani Ashish Joshi, Shivaprasad Bm, Shobana Anbu, Shohini Basu, Shravani N, Shravani Reddy, Shreya Anand, Shreya Kashyap, Shreya R, Shreya Vijoy Kumar, Shreyash Dwivedi, Shridhar Saraf, Shrimant, Shriram Gururaj Katti, Shriram Khushal Jadhav, Shristy Shrivastava, Shruthi T.s, Shruti Gupta, Shruti Hetal Gandhi, Shruti Pathak, Shruti Shukla, Shubhajyoti Sengupta, Shubham Hiremath, Shubham Singh, Shubham Singh Baghel, Shubham Suresh Basalwar, Shusovan Chakraborty, Shuvendu Kumar Dash, Shweta Kumari, Shwetha K T, Shwetha Kumari, Shwetha R, Shwetha R Murthy, Shwetha Ramesh, Shwetha S Kumar, Shyam Sidhu Murugesan, Shyla M V, Sibaprasad Mishra, Siddesh A S, Sidharth Mallik, Siiranjeevi, Silpa Chelluri, Sindhu Pulikizha Theril, Siranjeevi R, Sirisha Deshpande, Sivaramakrishna Yasarla, Sivaranjani P, Smriti Dixit, Sneha Anand, Sneha Mishra, Sneha Patnaik, Sneha Polaki, Snehal Harsh, Snehalata Patil, Snitha Suresh, Sohilkumar Amirbhai Shivani, Somaraju Venkata Naga Bhavani Sruti, Somya Sinha, Soubhagya

Mishra, Soubhagya Ranjan Pradhan, Soumita Guha, Soumya Roy, Soumya Shiddalingappa Khairawadagi, Soundarya S M, Soundarya V, Sourabh Choubey, Sourabh Suresh Kanchibail, Sourav Bhange, Sowmya Shree S.k, Sowrabha M, Spandana Athkuri Vani, Sravya Bogadapati, Sree Keerthi Pujari, Sreeja T, Sreelakshmi B.s, Sreenivasan Arunachalam, Sreenuraj Varma M, Sreesha Y S, Sreyas T J, Sri Raksha K, Srichitra Dulipala, Sridhar Krishna Mohan Panguluri, Srikanth Shenoy, Srinivas Kadiyala, Sripriya R, Srishti Sharma, Srishti Suman, Sritam Singh, Srivasavi M, Steffi Chinnu Thomas, Subash K, Subhashis, Subhashis Gobinda Baruah, Subhasis Nayak, Subhasis Pati, Subhendu Biswal, Subhrajyoti Mohapatra, Subramanya Rao Koteshwar, Subrata Dey, Suchintra Karan Singh, Suchismita Bindhani, Sudhir Reddy G, Suhas, Suhas A R, Suhas Agarwal, Suhas Mashal B, Suhel Firoz Mestri, Sujatha Reddy, Sukanya Rajendran, Suma S, Sumana Santra, Sumeet Shah, Sunil Kumar, Sunil Kumar T, Sunil Nagaraj, Sunita Yadav, Supreetha J, Supriya S, Supriya Satish Deshmukh, Suraj Mishra, Suraksha K S, Surendra Katperi, Suresh Kumar G, Suresh Nanjan, Sushant Jadhav, Sushant S Chapali, Sushanta Nandy, Sushen Patil, Sushil Pokharia, Sushmitha R, Sushmitha V, Sushmitha Vani, Sushree Sarkar, Susmitha Subramanya, Swapnil, Swarnalatha Karnam, Swarnanil Dasgupta, Swathi Bharadwaj, Swathi Bhardwaj, Swathy Venu K, Swetha Reddy, Swetha Srinivas Murthy, Syed Nawaz, Syed Rashid Pasha, Syed Rehman G, Syeda Nida Seher, Tanvi Sanjay Patil, Tanvi Sawant, Tapasya K Murdeshwar, Tarun K A, Tasmin Naim Khan Pathan, Teejo Joseph K J, Teja K, Tejas Pradeep Bhad, Thejesh K, Thejus R, Thiruvengadam S, Tripti Mishra, Tripti Shahi, Trupti Dadhich, Tuhin Chakraborty, Tumul Shyam Verma, Tushar Sharma, Udeepta Kashyap, Udit Bhola, Ujjwala Gorantla, Ulfath Joad, Ungarala Venkata Satya Durga Prasad, Usha P, Utkarsha Vijay Jadkar, Vaibhav Kaushik, Vaisakh V L, Vaishali Shrinivas Sawai, Vaishnavi Bhat D B, Vaka Ganesh, Vandana Raheja, Vanishree R, Varrsha Mohan Halkatti, Varsha R Budhihal, Varshith A, Vasu Venkatesh, Vathender B, Veda Prada, Veda Prada Nataraja, Vedanshi Sinha, Veena S Chincholi, Veena V, Veena V, Veerabhadraiah R, Venkat Kumar Nainala, Venkata Naga Bhavani Sruti Somaraju, Venkata Sudhakar Reddy, Venkatesh Kr, Venugopal, Vidisha Vaishnav, Vidya Krishna, Vidya Lakshmi S Shet, Vighnesh Pm, Vignesh Paramasivam, Vijay Ananda Chavan, Vijayakumari M, Vijayalakshmi, Vikash Kumar Pandey, Vikram K N, Vimal Kumar Ravi, Vinay Kumar, Vineeth Ravi, Vineth Kumar R, Vinita Gupta, Vinod Kumar, Vinod Kumar B S, Vinoth M,

Vinothini Ganesan, Vipin Vinchurkar, Vishal Rameshkumar, Vishal S, Vishala Bidlur Nagaraj, Vishalakshi Gv, Vishalkiran Reddy, Vivek Khamparia, Vivek Verma, Vrushab Patil, Vybhav, Vybhav Nv, Vyshak B S, Vyshak V, Yaddula Lakshminath Reddy, Yadhunandan R, Yalla Reddy, Yallanuru Venkateswarlu, Yashaswini Mohan, Yashodha K, Yasmeen Shoeb, Yatheendra B.c, Yogesh Jayaseelan, Yogesh Kumar Gujrati

Testing has this super power. It can be used for any purpose you deem fit.

We use testing to drive growth.

Growth is the only metric people sponsoring us is caring about.